Fish, Food, and Hunger

About the Book and Author

Because world hunger continues to be a critical issue in contemporary society, alternative food sources—as well as improved production, processing, and distribution methods—must be found. In this broadly based and thorough study, the author argues that fish production can make a significant contribution toward improving the food supply of impoverished people, serving as a possible remedy for malnutrition. Dr. Kent's suggestions for maximizing the potential of national and international fisheries to alleviate malnutrition are illustrated with case studies from the Philippines, Thailand, India, Southern Africa, and the Pacific Islands.

George Kent is professor of political science at the University of Hawaii and consultant to the Food and Agriculture Organization of the United Nations.

Fish, Food, and Hunger

The Potential of Fisheries for Alleviating Malnutrition

George Kent

Routledge
Taylor & Francis Group

LONDON AND NEW YORK

First published 1987 by Westview Press

Published 2018 by Routledge
52 Vanderbilt Avenue, New York, NY 10017
2 Park Square, Milton Park, Abingdon, Oxon OX14 4RN

Routledge is an imprint of the Taylor & Francis Group, an informa business

Library of Congress Cataloging-in-Publication Data
Kent, George, 1939–
    Fish, food, and hunger.
    (Westview special studies in ocean science and
policy)
    Bibliography: p.
    1. Fish trade.   2. Fisheries.   3. Food supply.
I. Title.   II. Series.
HD9450.5.K46   1987   338.3'7194   87-6066
ISBN 0-8133-7409-X

ISBN 13: 978-0-367-01391-2 (hbk)
ISBN 13: 978-0-367-16378-5 (pbk)

CONTENTS

PART 1

FISH AND NUTRITION

Chapter 1

INTRODUCTION

Many observers have suggested that the sea is a bountiful storehouse of food which could be used to help end hunger in the world.[1] The possibilities have sometimes been exaggerated, but there is no doubt that fish and other seafood could be used more effectively. The purpose of this study is to examine ways in which policies might be modified so that fisheries could make a greater contribution to the alleviation of malnutrition.

BACKGROUND

In 1975 a meeting on Expanding the Utilization of Marine Resources for Human Consumption was sponsored by the Norwegian Agency for International Development (NORAD). Another meeting sponsored by NORAD and the Food and Agriculture Organization of the United Nations (FAO) held in Malaysia in 1982 explored ways in which fuller use might be made of fishery products in developing countries.[2] Then an Expert Consultation on the Role of Fish and Fisheries in World Nutrition, organized by the government of Norway and sponsored by the FAO was held in Oslo in July 1983. I was invited to that meeting because my 1980 book on *The Politics of Pacific Islands Fisheries* included a chapter on nutritional aspects of fisheries. I was particularly pleased because, although my hosts had not known it, at the time I was writing *The Political Economy of Hunger: The Silent Holocaust*, which came out in 1984.

The core question at the 1983 Oslo meeting was "How can fisheries be managed and developed to be more effective in alleviating malnutrition?" Many possibilities were outlined, including actions by national governments, fishing communities, producers, research agencies, food assistance agencies, and development agencies. The consultation recommended that the role of fisheries in alleviating undernutrition be proposed as a specific action program for fisheries development at the upcoming World Fisheries Conference.[3] In October 1983 the FAO's Committee on Fisheries supported this recommendation and incorporated it into the Draft Strategy which was prepared for consideration by the FAO World Conference on Fisheries Management and Development held in the summer of 1984.[4] That conference endorsed the "Action Programme on the Promotion of the Role of Fisheries in Alleviating Undernutrition" without dissent.[5] The FAO's Fisheries Department is responsible for the implementation of the program, and cooperates closely with the FAO's Food Policy and Nutrition Division and the FAO/UN World Food Programme.

In the summer of 1984 I undertook a consultancy with the Fishery Industries Division of FAO to provide background on the major policy issues. This work resulted in a study on existing and potential linkages between national fisheries policies and national nutritional policies, with the Philippines and Thailand as the specific cases under examination.[6] The study reviewed their fisheries and nutrition situations and suggested ways in which policies in these countries might be reoriented to make a better contribution to the alleviation of undernutrition. With the support of the FAO, I did follow-up work directly with Thailand's Department of Fisheries in the summer of 1985. I prepared another paper on fisheries-nutrition linkages for an FAO-supported conference held in New Delhi in November 1985 and did follow-up work in India in the summer of 1986. These, together with several other studies I did on the theme, provided much of the material from which this book was prepared.

SCOPE

Fishery products are taken to include finfish and shellfish and the many different food products which can be derived from them. These products can be used to alleviate malnutrition either directly, through their consumption value, or indirectly, through their commodity value. Fishing people who sell their catch to buy other foods use the fish only indirectly for their personal nutrition; for them, the nutritive character of the product they sell is only incidental. In this study the focus is on the use of fish for its direct consumption value, not its commodity value.

Programs for the alleviation of malnutrition might be considered for several different kinds of problematic situations. First, it might be projected that in the long run the supply of particular foods will not grow fast enough to keep up with the demand, resulting in serious shortfalls.[7] Second, policymakers might be concerned with the possibility of famine, that is, episodic and possibly surprising shortfalls in food supplies which threaten immediate and severe dislocations.[8] Third, programs might be designed to respond to problems of chronic malnutrition, particularly the widespread, continuing malnutrition which affects substantial portions of the populations of many developing countries. This study addresses only the third of these possibilities.

Although others can be malnourished as well, the focus here is on the poor as the socioeconomic group most vulnerable to malnutrition.

This study focuses on a few selected countries and regions, but the intention is to provide background information and guidelines which would be useful anywhere there is some potential for using fisheries products to help in alleviating malnutrition.

Part 1 provides basic descriptive information on fisheries and on nutrition, and categorically outlines actions that could be taken to enhance the contribution of fisheries to the alleviation of malnutrition. Concrete applications of these ideas are surveyed on a national and regional basis in Part 2. Part 3 derives generalizations

6

regarding the evaluation and design of both fisheries projects and fisheries policies.

NOTES

1. Frederick W. Bell, *Food from the Sea: The Economics and Politics of Ocean Fisheries* (Boulder, Colorado: Westview Press, 1978); Clarence P. Idyll, *The Sea Against Hunger: Harvesting the Oceans to Feed a Hungry World*, Revised edition (New York: Thomas Y. Crowell Co., 1978); Claudia Carr and James Carr, "World Hunger: A Solution from the Sea?" *Environment*, Vol. 22, No. 1 (January 1980), p. 3.
2. Food and Agriculture Organization of the United Nations, *Fishery Products and the Consumer in Developing Countries*, FAO Fisheries Report No. 271 (Rome: FAO, 1982).
3. Food and Agriculture Organization of the United Nations, *The Potential of Fisheries in Alleviating Undernutrition: Report of the Discussions and Conclusions of an Expert Consultation on the Role of Fish and Fisheries in World Nutrition* (Rome: FAO, 1983).
4. FAO World Conference on Fisheries Management and Development, *Draft Strategy for Fisheries Management and Development and Associated Programs of Action* (Rome: FAO, 1984).
5. Food and Agriculture Organization of the United Nations, *Report of the FAO World Conference on Fisheries Management and Development, Rome 27 June to 6 July 1984* (Rome: FAO, 1984), pp. 50-52.
6. George Kent, *National Fisheries Policies and the Alleviation of Malnutrition in the Philippines and Thailand*,

FAO Fisheries Circular No. 777 (Rome: Food and Agriculture Organization of the United Nations, 1984).

7. M. A. Robinson, *Prospects for World Fisheries to 2000* (Rome: Food and Agriculture Organization of the United Nations, 1982).

8. This was the focus of the *FAO Workshop on National Preparedness for Acute and Large-Scale Food Shortages in Asia and the Pacific, Bangkok, 2-6 May 1983* (Rome: Food and Agriculture Organization of the United Nations, 1983).

Chapter 2

FISH IN THE WORLD FOOD SYSTEM

PATTERNS OF FISH CONSUMPTION

About 80 million tons of fish are produced (caught or cultured) globally each year. Almost 12 percent of this total comes from inland waters, while the rest is marine fish. Developed countries produce about 51 percent of the world catch while developing countries produce about 49 percent.

Although production is divided evenly between developed and developing countries, the consumption pattern is very different. As Frederick Bell observed, "the major consumers are affluent, not developing countries."[1] The pattern may be seen in Table 2.1. These data refer to total supplies of fish products for any given country, comprised of its production, plus its imports, minus its exports. Direct use refers to direct human consumption, while indirect use refers primarily to the use of fish as feed for livestock. About 27 percent of world production is used for fish meal, most of which is used as feed for pigs and poultry. As the table shows, the developed countries together use a bit more than half the world's fish.

The developed countries taken together have only about a third of the population of the less developed countries. Thus the differences in their consumption levels are much more marked when per capita measures are used. Table 2.1 shows that on a per capita basis people in developed countries use more than three times as much fish as people in developing countries--34 kilograms as

TABLE 2.1

Distribution of Food Originating from Fish and Fishery Products, 1980-1982

Country Shares		Per Capita Shares	
Direct Use	Direct and Indirect Use	Direct Use	Direct and Indirect Use
(% of world total)		(kg/capita/year, live weight equiv.)	
Developed Countries			
53.1	53.7	25.4	34.2
Developing Countries			
46.9	46.3	7.7	10.4

Note: These data refer to total supplies of fish products for each country, comprised of its production, plus its imports, minus its exports. Direct use refers to direct human consumption, while indirect use refers to feed for livestock and other non-food uses.

Source: Food and Agriculture Organization of the United Nations, *1984 Yearbook of Fishery Statistics: Fishery Commodities*, Vol. 59 (Rome: FAO, 1986), p. 253.

opposed to 10 kilograms. Even if there is underreporting of local consumption, it is evident that the disparity is substantial.

These data on distribution among countries do not show the further skew which results from the uneven distribution of resources within countries.

The trend is toward further widening of the gap in consumption levels. From 1973 to 1983 the world supply of fish for direct human consumption increased from 47 million to 60 million tons. In developing countries the fish supplied increased from 7 kg/year to 8 kg/year per capita, while in the developed countries the supply increased from 23 kg/year to 27 kg/year. Thus most of the increase went to developed countries.[2]

People in developed countries consume more fish, but they consume more of all kinds of food, so in terms of their nutrition they cannot be said to rely on that fish. People of less developed countries, however, tend to be far more dependent on fish because it accounts for a far higher proportion of their animal protein intake. As the former Assistant Director General for Fisheries of the FAO pointed out:

> Fish makes up roughly twenty percent of the world's total supply of animal protein, and for people of the developing world, it counts for much more than that. For over half of these people, fish supplies one third of the relatively meagre amount of animal protein they do get. In Africa it accounts for 24 percent of animal protein intake; in populous South East Asia 55 percent.[3]

In a more recent account:

> In 1979-81, fish provided 5.3% of total protein supplies at the world level, 4.3% in the developing, and 7.6% in the developed market economies. Its contribution to world supplies of animal protein was as much as 15%. Although the figure for the developed market economies was lower (13%), fish contributed no less than 20% of the meagre animal protein supplies of developing market economies.[4]

Fish contributes a large share of animal protein, but as shown in the following chapter, in poor countries animal protein accounts for a relatively small share of overall protein supplies. The question, then, is whether even small amounts of animal protein should be judged important.

FISH TRADE

The basic pattern of international trade in food is that most of the trade is among developed countries; there is little trade among the developing countries; and in the trade between the two groups, on balance food tends to flow from the less developed to the more highly developed countries. The net flow is upward, not downward.[5] The same pattern holds with respect to fish.[6] In 1984, about 12 million metric tons of fish entered into international trade. As Table 2.2 shows, developed countries exported 61.1 percent of this total, but imported 78.4 percent, thus taking out more than they put in. Developing countries exported 38.9 percent and imported 21.6 percent of the total quantity, putting in more than they took out.

Of course the pattern with respect to money is just the opposite. In 1984 the fisheries balance of trade (value of exports minus value of imports) for developing countries was about five billion dollars, which means they earned a good deal of foreign exchange. For developed countries the balance was minus five billion dollars, which means they spent much more than they earned from fisheries trade.

The pattern of fish trade may be seen from the perspective of individual countries. For the United States, fish imports have greatly exceeded exports, both by value and by weight, in every year since 1930. In 1985, for example, the United States exported 648,134,000 pounds of edible fish, valued at $1,010,268. In the same year the United States imported 2,754,018,000 pounds of edible fish, worth $4,064,346,000. In addition, in 1985 the United States exported $73,846,000 worth of nonedible fish products, and imported $2,614,252,000 worth of nonedible fish products.[7] The limited importance of commercial

TABLE 2.2

Shares in World Fish Trade, 1984
(percentage)

	Imports		Exports	
	Quantity	Value	Quantity	Value
Developed Countries				
	78.4	87.6	61.1	55.4
Developing Countries				
	21.6	12.4	38.9	44.6

Source: Food and Agriculture Organization of the United Nations, *1984 Yearbook of Fishery Statistics: Fishery Commodities*, Vol. 59. (Rome: FAO, 1986), pp. 26-27.

production is suggested by the fact that the recreational fishing industry "is by all measures economically more important in the United States than domestic commercial fishing for food!"[8]

As Table 2.3 shows, Japan too has been importing increasingly large quantities of fish:

> Japan used to be a fish-consuming nation and a major fish exporter at the same time. In 1971 Japan became a net importer in terms of value, and in 1975 it became a net importer in terms of volume. Since then, the excess of imports over exports has been rapidly increasing.[9]

The rapid rise of imports by Japan began well before the widespread extension of fisheries jurisdictions in the mid-1970s.

The flow of fish in the international market from less developed to more highly developed countries is indicated by the fact that most countries purchase their fish imports from countries which are poorer (in terms of gross national product per capita) than those to which they send their fish exports.[10]

Another indication that the flow tends to be from the poor to the rich is that in the trade in simply preserved fish (for example, frozen), among the market economies of the world, developed countries export around 70 percent but import 90 percent of the total value of fish traded.

The Organisation for Economic Co-operation and Development (OECD) plainly acknowledges the pattern:

> Statistics of world trade in sea products show the very strong preponderance of OECD countries, which in value terms account for 85 per cent of imports and 59 per cent of exports. That is to say, the main flow of exported fish and fish products is, irrespective of country of origin, towards more advanced and better nourished nations.[11]

Thus fish continue to migrate after they are caught. They tend to flow from the more needy to the less needy.

TABLE 2.3

Japanese Fish Trade
(thousands of tons; millions of yen)

	Exports		Imports	
Year	Quantity	Value	Quantity	Value
1960	---	84,212	47	5,523
1965	565	118,997	279	37,422
1970	579	140,718	375	114,628
1975	603	168,696	710	385,529
1977	591	184,180	1046	657,714
1978	754	171,250	1018	676,455
1979	728	196,363	1151	930,764

Source: Japanese External Trade Organization, *Japanese Fisheries Trade and Trade in Fishery Products* (Tokyo: JETRO, 1981), p. 33.

One very clear illustration is provided by the fact that 56 million pounds of fish were exported from the famine stricken Sahel region of Africa in 1971 alone.

It is sometimes suggested that if anchoveta or shrimp or some other product were not exported it would not be used at all, and thus would be wasted. After all, before India discovered the lucrative world market for it, shrimp in India was simply discarded or used as fertilizer. This argument fails to acknowledge that the raw resource is only one of many inputs into food production. Export-oriented production often diverts labor, capital and other resources away from production for local consumption.

It is sometimes argued that certain products must be exported because local people have no taste for them. For example, it is said that Pacific islanders prefer imported canned mackerel to the tuna that is caught and canned on their own shores. There is some truth to this, but the argument is commonly overstated. The tuna sold in local markets in the Pacific islands is generally of the lowest grade--tuna flakes which would be sold as pet food in the United States--and it appears in the local markets at perhaps twice the price of mackerel. The higher grades of tuna are exported, not because there is no taste for them locally, but because rich countries are willing and able to pay more for them.

The fish and other food which moves in international trade is only a small share of the total amount of food produced and consumed. But the pattern of the poor feeding the rich is found within as well as among nations. The thesis that the poor feed the rich is not only about international relations; it is about social structures based on the market system wherever they occur. This regular flow of fish and other food toward the top, within countries as well as among countries, helps to account for the chronic undernutrition at the bottom.

THE EDIBILITY QUESTION

The share of fish consumption in developed countries that is accounted for by imports is higher if non-

edible fishery products are included. The determination
of what is edible is not a simple technical question.
Products that may be regarded as nonedible when they
reach developed countries, and thus relegated to feed, frequently are regarded as edible at the point of origin. A
case from Africa illustrates this:

> In Senegal . . . there exists a factory for the
> production of fishmeal. . . . This factory,
> Sopesine, owned by two French companies . . .
> treats 2800 tonnes of sardines each year (fish fit
> for human consumption) in order to produce . . .
> fish meal and oil. Ninety-five percent of the fish
> meal is destined for consumption by French live-
> stock. . . . One hundred kilometers from [the
> landing area] peasants don't eat fish because it is
> not available or it is too expensive.[12]

Products regarded as substantial food resources by
the poor may be used for feed for pigs and poultry for
the rich, or may be used to feed their pets:

> . . . a cheap Moroccan canned fish, developed for
> the Middle East markets, primarily Egypt, brought a
> higher price when sold to the United States as cat
> food. One third of the canned fish of the United
> States is in effect pet food. An equally large por-
> tion of the British output of canned fish is devoted
> to the same purpose. In most instances this con-
> stitutes food which would be very much in demand
> if offered to the protein-needy and malnourished
> around the globe.[13]

The argument that the product is not suitable for
direct human consumption has been used to defend the export of anchoveta from Latin America to western Europe
and Japan to feed pigs and poultry. Actually, instead of
being converted to fishmeal for animal feed the anchoveta
technically could be converted to fish protein concentrate
for human consumption. Even if livestock feed were the
only possible use for these sardines and anchoveta, there
would still remain the question of why the feed should be

consumed by livestock used by Europeans rather than by Africans or Latin Americans.

THE PROBLEMS

On balance there is a net flow of fish from poor countries to rich countries, but why should this be viewed as problematic? The rich countries do pay for the fish they get. Obviously both sides benefit from the transactions, for otherwise either of them could simply refuse to participate.

There are three major concerns, all of which require further research.

The first concern is that in the fisheries trade (as in other kinds of trade) the richer trading partners are likely to get a larger share of benefits than the poorer trading partners. In the tuna and shrimp industries, for example, the processors and marketers in the rich countries are likely to obtain far higher benefits than the suppliers in the poor countries.[14] Thus, while both sides gain some benefit, the relationship contributes to the widening of the gap between rich and poor, with the poor lagging further and further behind.

Devoting local resources to production for export requires increased dependence on imports. The net result can be that apparent gains are dissipated by inflation and by disadvantageous terms of trade, and there can be a great buildup of external debt. The Philippines under the Marcos government faced this problem:

> The Philippine government is currently pursuing a policy of production for export. With reference to Japan, this policy is particularly urgent in order to offset the record $355 million total trade deficit the Philippines incurred in 1976. In the fishing industry, such a policy is questionable as local demand for fish has yet to be met, and most Filipinos have been made to do with a diet of low quality fish as the better kinds are now beyond their means.[15]

The problem was further exacerbated in the late 1970s and early 1980s with the great emphasis on tuna production for export.[16]

This raises the second concern: the foreign exchange that is earned from the export of fisheries products from poor countries may not be used where it is needed most. The point is illustrated by a group of Indian fishermen:

> To add to our country's misery, the developed world is now making strident demands for our other varieties of fish, like sardines, tuna, mackerels and pomphrets which have also been promoted as delicacies in their countries. If this trend continues the Indian population will have to do without fish since the foreign buyers are ready to pay ten times the amount of money a poor Indian could hardly afford. Can we allow our fish which is our vital food resources to be exported at the cost of the protein-starved population of our country; even if the principle involved is the highly questionable foreign exchange earnings?[17]

Often there is some compensation for increasing exports by the increasing imports of food. More typically, however, the foreign exchange earned from the export of food is not devoted to purchasing low cost nutritive foods for the needy, but is diverted to the purchase of luxury foods and other products in demand by local elites.

A favorable balance of trade in money certainly can compensate for an unfavorable balance in terms of nutrition. But whether it can compensate and whether it does in fact compensate are two different questions. Further research on the question is needed, but on the basis of the high levels of undernutrition and on the basis of the composition and magnitudes of imports in many less developed countries, it appears that foreign exchange earnings frequently are not used to meet basic nutritional needs.

The third concern is that in a world in which there are more than 500 million people who are significantly malnourished, it simply does not make sense to export major food supplies away from those who do not have enough.

Rich countries use more fish than they produce, with the difference made up by imports. Georg Borgstrom has commented:

> No doubt everyone realizes how preposterous it is that the two most protein-needy continents, Africa and South America, are the main suppliers of the largest quantities of animal protein feed moving in the world trade--and they provide those who already have plenty. . . . The Peruvian catches alone would suffice to raise the nutritional standard with respect to protein for the undernourished on the entire South American continent to southern European level. The amount of protein extracted (1966-68) exceeds by one half the meat protein produced in South America and is three times the milk protein raised. The corresponding fish meal coming from Africa would be enough to reduce by at least 50 per cent the present protein shortage of that continent.[18]

An FAO expert has observed that:

> . . . there is a disturbing trend in fish consumption. Increases in fish production have gone primarily to those countries that could afford to pay. The average *per caput* consumption in developing market economies has increased but by only 600 g since 1960, while in Eastern Europe and the USSR *per caput* consumption rose about 12 kg and, in other developed countries, by 3.5 kg. This trend is alarming because it indicates the potential danger that an increasing share of world catch will be siphoned off to the higher purchasing power in developed areas and by the centrally planned economies, leaving less fish where it is much needed--in the developing regions.[19]

Many poor countries export food despite their suffering serious malnutrition at home. Brazil, Chile,

Ecuador, India, Mauritania, Morocco, Peru, Senegal, and Thailand, for example, all suffer widespread malnutrition but at the same time are net exporters of fish. Of course it is possible that the foreign exchange that is earned from exporting fish is used to help alleviate what might be even worse conditions of undernutrition in these countries. Nevertheless, this pattern of export of fish from countries which suffer significant undernutrition warrants further investigation.

In Thailand, Malaysia, and the Philippines seafood exports have expanded sharply while at the same time local consumption of this major protein source has declined. In Malaysia the quantity of fish available per person in 1975 was 30 percent lower than the 1967 level, despite the fact that the total catch increased substantially. Most of the increase in production has been exported. The situation in Thailand is similar:

> In 1972, the total fish catch in Thailand was 1.55 million tons. It fell slightly in the next few years and returned to 1.6 million tons by 1977. Yet seafood exports boomed, though the local catch had barely changed in five years and the population had grown.[20]

Thailand is certainly not exporting only the surplus which remains after domestic needs are fulfilled. The indications are that local consumption is sacrificed for exports.

To see what is problematic about the upstream trade in fish one should go beyond the merely economic and acknowledge that it is important to fulfill needs as well as to meet market demand.

REMEDIES

Scientists often voice the hope that fisheries products might someday make an important contribution toward meeting the problems of malnutrition in the world. Agencies like the FAO or the United States National Academy of Sciences urge the development of new technologies and the opening of new and exotic fisheries.[21] Their recommendations make sense with respect to the conventional motivation of maximizing revenues and perhaps as a means of maximizing total quantities produced. But what are the prospects that the approaches they recommend would result in an effective response to the problem of world hunger?

Those who press for the opening of new stocks or for research and development leading to new technological breakthroughs have missed the message already very clearly established in the history of agriculture. It is in the nature of the prevailing modes of management that any newly developed resource or new technological breakthroughs are likely to be used to the advantage of the already advantaged.

The research and development agenda is consistently skewed in favor of revenue-producing products and projects and gives little support to efforts distinguished by their nutritional importance. For example, reef fishing and the gleaning of shellfish from drying reefs have received little attention because they are not of commercial importance, despite the fact that often they are significant for local nutrition. Whether in small-scale or large-scale fisheries development efforts, full attention is given to the money value of the product but almost no attention is given to its nutritive value.

Prevailing research priorities are suggested by the fact that in the bibliographic section of fisheries newsletters, the section on nutrition is about the feeding of aquaculture species, not about human nutrition. Whether in connection with agriculture or aquaculture, far more of the world's nutrition research is about the feeding of livestock than about human nutrition. Of that research which is about human nutrition, very little is about malnutrition. Much more attention should be given to the ways in which fisheries projects might make larger contributions to the alleviation of malnutrition.

Simply increasing overall fish supplies in itself is unlikely to help very much because in the absence of special measures most of the product is likely to go to those who already have enough. And while trade can be beneficial to all trading partners, it is likely to be much more beneficial to the richer partner. Pursued indiscriminately, increasing trade can promote the widening of the gap between the rich and the poor and thus help to promote rather than alleviate chronic undernutrition.

There are some promising ways in which fisheries could be managed to be more responsive to the problem of chronic undernutrition.

Institutional linkages between agencies responsible for health and nutrition and agencies responsible for fisheries management should be strengthened. International agencies could take the lead by giving more attention to the potentials of fisheries for addressing problems of undernutrition. In supporting fisheries development projects, one of the Asian Development Bank's principal aims is "to increase the availability of fish and fish products for domestic consumption."[22] But providing fish for general consumption is quite different from responding to the particular problems of those who are seriously undernourished. The lack of focus on this point is suggested by the fact that the ADB lists a wide range of "Issues for Fisheries Development," but the problem of undernutrition is not among them.

The World Bank also has been insensitive to the problem. The bank acknowledges that "small-scale fisheries provide most of the fish consumed by people in developing countries," and at the same time reports that in the twenty-seven fishing projects funded between 1964 and 1981 "the major objective has been to increase production for export. Nearly 60 % of the loans were utilized for large-scale fishery development."[23]

The South China Sea Project in Manila (now defunct), the Pacific Tuna Development Foundation (now the Pacific Fisheries Development Foundation), the Southeast Asia Fisheries Development Center (SEAFDEC) and other fisheries development agencies, having focused on large-scale operations for export, have been subjected to similar criticisms. Many of these agencies, including the World Bank, are now giving more attention to small-scale fisheries. However, the orientation remains primarily commercial. There is still very little attention being given to the actual and potential relationships between fisheries and undernutrition.

Although it cannot guarantee that supplies go to those most in need, increasing food self-reliance at the regional, national, and community levels can be very helpful. Increasingly, emphasis should be placed on local production for local consumption. Trading loops should be shortened so that fisheries become more responsive to local rather than alien interests. To the extent that they promote trade among less developed countries, agencies such as the FAO's Fish Marketing Information and Advisory Services could be very helpful.

Increasing self-reliance among developed countries would help as well. Rich countries could help poor countries to become more self-reliant by increasing their own food self-reliance--that is, by reducing the amount of food they import.

The export orientation of local fisheries can be reduced through the imposition of export taxes. The outflow of fish also can be limited in other ways. In Malaysia, in order to increase supplies to local consumers, trucks have been required to unload 10 percent of their load in Johore before going on to Singapore. Import duties can be used to reduce the inflow of fish from outside. For example, instead of continuing to import large quantities of canned mackerel from Japan, Papua New Guinea could place duties on imports and support the creation of its own domestic mackerel processing industry, based on the ample stocks found off its own shores.

So long as the Japanese are able to deliver mackerel extraordinarily cheaply, the creation of a domestic mackerel industry might not be warranted in commercial terms. But there might be other justifications for launching such an enterprise. Food security might be a major consideration. It might be wise to expand the domestic fish supply in order to become more independent of the vagaries of outside markets and outside forces. The industry might be used to create jobs in production, processing, and marketing. The product might be used not only for regular commercial marketing but also for subsidized programs specifically directed to the seriously undernourished.

The argument here is not that nations should undertake projects that are uneconomic, but rather that they should broaden the range of values taken into consideration in designing fisheries development projects, taking particular account of basic nutritional needs. If fisheries projects are judged exclusively by narrow market standards they will not be responsive to the problem of chronic undernutrition. Capital can be invested in and generate a profit in the production of foods for the poor, but generally that capital is likely to generate an even larger return when invested in production for the middle or upper classes. Thus, in any enterprise designed to produce food for the poor, one must be willing to forgo the maximization of profit and instead optimize, taking other values into account as well.

No one advocates that fisheries should be wholly devoted to alleviating undernutrition. There are several other valid social purposes such as generation of incomes, foreign exchange, and employment opportunities, which fisheries can and should serve as well. The question is, how might some redirection be achieved? The following chapters describe prospects in several different kinds of contexts.

However, before appropriate strategies can be designed, there must be a recognition of the realities of malnutrition in specific communities and of the potential for using fisheries in addressing those problems. Methods and techniques would vary according to circumstances, but there will be no action in this direction at all if there is no motivation for it.

NOTES

1. Frederick W. Bell, *Food from the Sea: The Economics and Politics of Ocean Fisheries* (Boulder, Colorado: Westview Press, 1978), p. 68.

2. Frans Teutscher, "Fish, Food and Human Nutrition," *Food and Nutrition*, Vol. 12, No. 2 (1986), pp. 2-10.
3. Kenneth C. Lucas, "World Fisheries Management: A Time to Build," *Vital Speeches of the Day*, XLV (1979), pp. 740-744.
4. Food and Agriculture Organization of the United Nations, *The Fifth World Food Survey* (Rome: FAO, 1985), p. 13.
5. George Kent, "Food Trade: The Poor Feed the Rich," *Food and Nutrition Bulletin*, Vol. 4, No. 4 (October 1982), pp. 25-33.
6. George Kent, "The Pattern of Fish Trade," *ICLARM Newsletter*, Vol. 6, No. 2 (April 1983), pp. 12-13.
7. National Marine Fisheries Service, *Imports and Exports of Fishery Products, Annual Summary 1985* (Washington, D.C.: NMFS, 1986), p. 10.
8. Bell, *Food from the Sea*, p. xxii.
9. Japan Information Service, "Japan's Imports of Fish Increase," *Japan Reports*, XXVI (1980), p. 3.
10. George Kent, *The Politics of Pacific Islands Fisheries* (Boulder, Colorado: Westview Press, 1980), pp. 87-92.
11. Organisation for Economic Co-operation and Development, *International Trade in Fish Products: Effects of the 200-Mile Limit* (Paris: OECD, 1982), p. 7.
12. CIDEPA--International Center for the Development of Fishing and Marine Cultivation, "Senegal--The Food Aid of the Third World to the Developed Countries is in Good Health," *For a Society Overcoming Domination: International Study Days, Case Study 110*, Paris: Support Service for Intercommunication, 1980.
13. Georg Borgstrom, *Too Many: A Study of the Earth's Biological Limitations* (New York: Macmillan, 1969), pp. 229-230.
14. George Kent, *Transnational Corporations in Pacific Fishing* (Sydney: Transnational Corporations Research Project, 1980).
15. Third World Studies, "Japanese Interests in the Philippines Fishing Industry," *AMPO: Japan-Asia Quarterly Review*, Vol. 10 (1978), pp. 52-60.

16. F. H. Magno, "Filipino's Per Capita Fish Intake Still Below Par," *Times Journal* (Manila), August 14, 1982, p. 6.
17. National Forum for Catamaran & Country-Boat Fishermen's Rights & Marine Wealth, India--"Ban Anti-National Multi-Million Fishing Complex at Colaba, Bombay, or Anywhere Else in India," *For a Society Overcoming Domination: International Study Days.* Case Study 1122 (Paris: Support Service for Intercommunication, 1980).
18. Borgstrom, *Too Many*, p. 237.
19. Paul Lunven, "The Role of Fish in Human Nutrition," *Food and Nutrition*, Vol. 8 (1982), pp. 9-18.
20. Ho Kwon Ping, "Profits and Poverty in the Plantations," *Far Eastern Economic Review*, Vol. 11 (1980), pp. 53-57.
21. National Academy of Sciences, *Supporting Papers: World Food and Nutrition Study*, Volume I (Washington, D.C.: NAS, 1977), pp. 251-318.
22. Asian Development Bank, *Bank Operations in the Fisheries Sector* (Manila: ADB, 1979).
23. World Bank, *Fishery Sector Policy Paper* (Washington, D.C.: WB, 1982).

Chapter 3

THE NUTRITIVE VALUE OF FISH

NUTRIENTS

Fish is a good source of readily digested, high quality animal protein.[1] It is high in lysine and sulphur amino acids which makes it particularly suitable for complementing the high carbohydrate diets prevailing in many less developed countries. The protein quality of fish assessed in terms of net protein utilization (the proportion of nitrogen intake that is retained in the body) is lower than that for hen eggs but similar to that in chicken, meat, milk, and cheese.[2] Most fish contains around 15 to 20 percent protein by weight.

Although it is most important as a source of protein, fish also has value as an energy source. Its contribution has been quite small. As Table 3.1 shows, in the Asia-Pacific region in 1980-82 there were ten countries in which fish contributed less than one percent of the total calorie consumption. Japan was the highest consumer of fish in the region, drawing over 7 percent of its dietary energy from seafood.

Fish provides preformed vitamin A and vitamin D if its oil is ingested. It is also a good source of minerals such as phosphorus, calcium, and iron. Fish bones, which may be eaten in small fish such as sardines, are particularly rich in calcium.[3] Marine species are a good source of iodine.

Fish is high in polyunsaturated fatty acids (especially omega-3) which can be important in lowering blood cholesterol levels. Evidence is accumulating that fatty fish may be highly effective in lowering blood pressure and preventing cardiovascular diseases. There also are

TABLE 3.1

Contribution of Fish to Total Dietary Energy Intake

Country	Contribution of Fish to Total Energy Intake (% of total calories)	Contribution of Fish to Energy Intake from Animal Products (% of calories from animal products)
Australia	0.71	2.33
Bangladesh	0.75	24.56
Burma	1.10	27.37
China	0.40	6.41
Dem. Kampuchea	0.96	26.76
D.P.R. Korea	2.32	39.44
Fiji	2.77	30.08
India	0.25	6.02
Indonesia	1.01	44.44
Japan	7.32	37.91
Laos	0.36	4.00
Malaysia	3.19	25.47
Maldives	5.49	89.60
Mongolia	0.07	0.24
New Zealand	0.34	0.99
Pakistan	0.18	2.31
Papua New Guinea	0.73	8.82
Philippines	2.79	30.73
Rep. of Korea	2.52	33.48
Samoa, Western	3.60	21.31
Sri Lanka	1.45	34.78
Thailand	1.56	25.71
Tonga	1.76	13.19
Vanuatu	3.21	16.00
Vietnam	1.14	19.51

Source: Food and Agriculture Organization of the United Nations, Regional Office for Asia and the Pacific, *Food Consumption in the Asia-Pacific Region 1972-1982* (Bangkok: FAO, RAPA, 1985), p. 17.

some indications that certain fatty acids in fish may provide protection against renal disease.[4]

OTHER VALUES

Apart from the specific nutrients it can provide, fish has a number of other distinctive qualities. Many find its taste and texture to be quite attractive. It is easily cooked and readily digested. In some places fish is viewed as a prestige food. It is familiar and highly acceptable in many parts of the world, particularly in less developed countries. It is widely available. As a flavoring it can help to make rice and other bland foods more palatable, and thus facilitate the consumption of larger quantities. Fatty fish eaten with green leafy vegetables can facilitate the metabolization of vitamin A from the vegetables. Fish is generally free of contaminants, particularly of the kinds of chemicals which are sometimes used to produce meat.[5]

On a unit weight basis, fish is expensive in comparison to vegetables and grains, but it is frequently less costly than alternative animal protein sources. In relation to its nutritional value it is relatively inexpensive, especially in some of its processed forms.

The major disadvantage of fish is its high perishability in its fresh form. However there are numerous ways in which it can be processed to reduce its perishability. Processing can not only reduce its perishability but also increase its attractiveness and its convenience for use. However, processing can be costly and it may entail some loss of nutrients.

Ironically, increasing awareness of the nutritional qualities of fisheries products could result in there being less available for the poor. "The US trend to increase consumption of lower calorie, lighter and more natural and nutritious foods favors the increased use of seafood,"[6] which means increasing demands on fisheries resources by middle and upper classes.

WORLD MALNUTRITION

According to the World Health Organization the deficiency diseases deserving the highest global priority are:

(a) PCM [protein-calorie or protein-energy malnutrition], because of its high mortality rate, its wide prevalence, and the irreversible physical and sometimes mental damage it may cause;

(b) xerophthalmia, because of its contribution to the mortality of malnourished children, its relatively wide prevalence, and the permanent blindness it causes;

(c) nutritional anemias, because of their wide distribution, their contribution to mortality from many other conditions, and their effects on working capacity; and

(d) endemic goiter, because of its wide distribution.[7]

Xerophthalmia results primarily from vitamin A deficiency, anemia from iron deficiency, and goiter from iodine deficiency.

The form of protein-energy malnutrition of primary concern here is chronic undernutrition, the debilitating malnutrition which is prevalent in a more or less steady state for substantial segments of the developing world, and also for smaller segments of developed societies.

The FAO's *Fourth World Food Survey* offered "an order of magnitude of about 400 million as a conservative estimate of the number of persons undernourished in the developing countries, excluding the Asian centrally planned economies."[8] The *Fifth World Food Survey* said that, depending on the criterion used, there were between 335 million and 494 million people in developing countries who were undernourished in 1979-81.[9]

The World Bank estimates that in 1980 about 340 million people did not get enough energy to prevent stunted growth and serious health risks. About 730 million did not get enough energy to sustain an active working life.[10]

Malnutrition strikes children especially hard. According to the United Nations Children's Fund (UNICEF), in 1981 about 17 million children died, and malnutrition was probably a contributing factor in a majority of these cases.[11]

Estimates of the numbers who are malnourished are calculated on the basis of energy deficiencies. Low protein intakes tend to be closely correlated with energy deficiencies. As Table 3.2 shows, people in developing countries obtain considerably smaller daily rations of protein, especially from animal sources.

THE POTENTIAL OF FISH

Protein-energy malnutrition usually results from a lack of energy foods, not protein. The apparent protein deficit commonly observed in cases of severe malnutrition results from the fact that the protein that is obtained is diverted to fulfilling immediate energy needs, and thus is not available for the body building and maintenance functions normally fulfilled by protein. In many circumstances needs can be fulfilled with cheap energy foods rather than with more expensive animal protein.[12]

In some cases, however, there is a genuine protein deficit, particularly where diets consist almost exclusively of cereals, and little animal or vegetable protein. Where the quantity and variety of vegetable sources consumed is not sufficient to provide an adequate intake of all essential amino acids, animal protein supplies (including dairy products) may be of critical importance.

Protein requirements in developing countries may be regularly underestimated:

> International standards . . . take into account variation in a normal population but are not adjusted for the protein quality of the actual diets consumed in developing countries. Moreover, they provide no allowance for the effects of infection . . . and other

Table 3.2

Daily Protein Supplies in Developed and Developing Countries, Per Capita (grams)

	1961-63	1964-66	1969-71	1972-74
Total Protein				
Developed market economies				
	90	91	94	95
Developing market economies				
	53	53	55	53
Animal Protein				
Developed market economies				
	48	50	55	56
Developing market economies				
	11	11	12	11

Source: Food and Agriculture Organization of the United Nations, *The Fourth World Food Survey* (Rome: FAO, 1977), p. 18.

adverse environmental factors experienced by populations of developing countries.[13]

Developed countries which set their own standards usually set their protein requirement levels higher than the international standards commonly applied to developing countries. Given the greater incidence of infectious diseases in developing countries, it should be recognized that their requirements for protein intake really are higher than those for developed countries.

It is recognized that the distribution of food within households is often skewed in favor of adult males and against women and children. But it is not so well known that the distribution of highly-valued animal products is likely to be skewed even more. For example, in refugee camps on the Thailand-Kampuchea border:

> When youngsters in the hospital were provided with pre-cooked gruels containing meat or fish, mothers would carefully pick these out before allowing the child to eat. The saved morsels of fish or meat were then given to other family members.[14]

Robert Orr Whyte has observed that "when children participate in adult meals it is common in Asia to deny them fish and egg."[15] More recently, a study of food distribution within the household conducted in Bangladesh showed that protein intake for adult males exceeded their requirements by 35 per cent while the intakes for women and children were below their requirements.[16]

The reconsideration of the importance of protein in the diet in the 1970s may have led to too great an emphasis on the importance of energy foods in response to malnutrition. However, "it is now apparent that added protein quantity or quality, when the protein value of a diet is inadequate, does bring about nutritional benefit whether or not calories are also inadequate."[17]

A report by the FAO's Committee on Agriculture acknowledges that "the poor usually cannot afford animal products in their diet" but then adds:

However, a notable exception is constituted by fish products which have remarkable effects in improving the monotony of the diet, and in providing high protein supplements. This is particularly true for young children who often cannot derive sufficient protein from crop products even when their stomachs are full, because of the bulkiness of the product. Dried fish is to be found in parts of the world remote from water sources and where it is often available at a low price. It then becomes an important constituent of the diets of malnourished children.[18]

In poor countries with abundant fisheries resources the contribution of fish to energy supplies might be increased substantially. It can be difficult to get sufficient energy from rice and other bulky carbohydrates, especially for small children. With its high nutrient density, fish--especially oily fish--can make an important contribution to the energy supplies of people at risk of malnutrition.

Fish may be particularly valuable for children:

In Jamaica, fish teas made from the mackaback (*Diapterus rhombeus* or *D. olithotomus*) could sometimes be afforded by poor mothers living not too far from the sea. In this, a fine puree is made of the whole of this sprat-sized fish, only the large bones being ultimately sieved off. In parts of South-East Asia, fish and shrimp pastes can be introduced in small amounts in the latter part of the first year of life just as in Thailand fish caught in the klongs are mixed with rice and given to older infants. Certain other sea-food preparations have been advocated . . . , among them various locally prepared fish and shrimp products--such as fish sauces, including the "nuoc mam" of Indo-China and the "nam pla" of Thailand, and fish pastes, such as the "bagoong" of the Philippines and the "trassi" ("terasi") of Indonesia and Malaya. (The last may also be made out of prawn's eggs.) It would seem that these might form valuable supplements of protein, calcium, and vitamin B_{12} for the older infant, although their strong flavor and admixed salt and condiments might render them unsuitable.[19]

Increased fish consumption by children may be beneficial in areas where lactose intolerance is common or where milk is expensive or in short supply. In the Philippines, for example, 98 percent of the milk supply is imported, which means that it is very expensive. In mid-1984 the lack of foreign exchange threatened the Philippines with a complete cutoff of its milk supply.[20]

Since small children are highly vulnerable to malnutrition, it would be useful to promote the use of fish as a weaning food. However, there are obstacles to increasing the consumption of fish by children, such as the fear held in Southeast Asia that eating fish can cause intestinal worms and the fear that children might choke on fish bones. In some cultures fish is boiled down before being fed to children, and in others the fish meat is handled vigorously to break it into smaller pieces and at the same time assure that there are no bones in it.

Apart from its energy and protein value, fish contains good amounts of vitamin A, iron, and iodine. Thus fish can be used to help remedy all four of the major forms of malnutrition identified by WHO.

Marine fish is particularly rich in iodine, and thus should be promoted in areas in which goiter is a problem, such as in central Java. If the supply from marine fish is inadequate, or if only freshwater fish is available, it might be possible to use iodized salt to salt fish. The effectiveness of such a strategy would need to be assessed.

Fish can be a good source of vitamin A. Where vitamin A deficiency is prevalent, the first line of attack normally would be to promote increased use of green leafy vegetables and other readily available foods which are rich in vitamin A. In some cases synthetic concentrated vitamin A may be provided in capsule form. However, where these are not suitable, fishery products may be helpful.

One approach to using fish for vitamin A is simply through the consumption of ordinary fish flesh. Greater concentrations can be obtained by eating the head as well.[21]

Second, the consumption of fatty fish along with green leafy vegetables can help in metabolizing vitamin A from the vegetables.

Third, oil from the livers of large fish is high in vitamin A, and can be taken in capsule doses. Traditionally, cod liver oil has been used for this purpose, but the liver oil from other species can be used as well. The "cod" liver oil available at the health centers in Bangkok is actually shark liver oil.

Fourth, specialty products such as shrimp paste are very high in vitamin A. The difficulty is that such products generally are taken only in small quantities, especially by children.

However, in most cases vitamin A deficiency does not occur in isolation but appears as part of overall protein-energy malnutrition. It usually makes more sense to work toward improving the diet as a whole than to focus on the particular vitamin deficiency. Fish can be a significant part of such broad programs.

Of course the appropriateness of fishery products for alleviating any sort of nutritional deficiency depends on particular local circumstances, taking into consideration issues such as their acceptability, availability, and cost in relation to alternative sources of the required nutrients.

NOTES

1. Eirik Heen and Rudolf Kreuzer, eds., *Fish in Nutrition* (London: Fishing News [Books] Ltd., 1962), and Georg Borgstrom, ed., *Fish as Food*, 4 vols. (New York: Academic Press, 1961, 1962, 1965, 1965) are two excellent anthologies providing detailed technical information on the nutritive qualities of fish. Only

the most important characteristics are reviewed here.

2. Sidney Holt, "Marine Fisheries," in Elisabeth Mann Borgese and Norton Ginsburg, eds., *Ocean Yearbook 1* (Chicago: University of Chicago Press, 1978), p. 66.
3. The Japanese are producing calcium from skipjack bones. Its largest outlet is in the school lunch program. See Masayoshi Sada, "Fish Calcium," *INFOFISH Marketing Digest*, No. 1/84 (January/February 1984), pp. 29-30.
4. William E. M. Lands, *Fish and Human Health* (Orlando, Florida: Academic Press, 1986). In late 1986 the Squibb pharmaceutical company began marketing "Proto-Chol" capsules "to add extra omega-3 oil to your total cholesterol-control program."
5. Orville Schell, *Modern Meat* (New York: Random House, 1984).
6. Joseph W. Slavin, "Review of US Seafood Market," *INFOFISH Marketing Digest*, No. 2/84 (March/April 1984), p. 22.
7. James E. Austin, *Confronting Urban Malnutrition: The Design of Nutrition Programs* (Baltimore: Johns Hopkins University Press/World Bank, 1980), p. 119.
8. Food and Agriculture Organization of the United Nations, *The Fourth World Food Survey* (Rome: FAO, 1977), p. 51.
9. Food and Agriculture Organization of the United Nations, *The Fifth World Food Survey* (Rome: FAO, 1985), p. 24.
10. World Bank, *Poverty and Hunger: Issues and Options for Food Security in Developing Countries* (Washington, D.C.: WB, 1986), p. 1.
11. James P. Grant, *The State of the World's Children 1981-82* (New York: United Nations Children's Fund, 1982).
12. D. S. McLaren, "The Great Protein Fiasco," *Lancet*, Vol. 2 (1974), pp. 93-96.
13. Gerald Keusch and Nevin S. Scrimshaw, "Control of Infection to Reduce Malnutrition," in Julia Walsh and Kenneth Warren (eds.), *Strategies for Primary*

40

Health Care (Chicago: University of Chicago Press, 1986).

14. Sheryl Keller, *Protein Revisited: Subclinical Protein Deficiency as a Significant Public Health Concern* (Honolulu: Unpublished manuscript, University of Hawaii, 1986.)

15. Robert Orr Whyte, *Rural Nutrition in Monsoon Asia* (London: Oxford University Press, 1974), p. 120.

16. Nazmul Hassan and Kamaluddin Ahmad, "Intra-familial Distribution of Food in Rural Bangladesh," *Food and Nutrition Bulletin*, Vol. 6, No. 4 (1984), pp. 34-42.

17. Nevin Scrimshaw, "Changing Nutritional Criteria and Absolute Poverty," *Development: Seeds of Change*, Vol. 4 (1982), p. 38.

18. Food and Agriculture Organization of the United Nations, Committee on Agriculture, *Malnutrition: Its Nature, Magnitude and Policy Implications* (Rome: FAO, COAG, December 1982), p. 6.

19. Derrick B. Jelliffe, *Infant Nutrition in the Subtropics and Tropics* (Geneva: World Health Organization, 1968), pp. 193-194.

20. "Milk Lack Threatens," *Times Journal* (Manila), July 29, 1984, pp. 1, 6.

21. According to the National Institute of Nutrition, *Annual Report, 1984-85* (New Delhi: Indian Council of Medical Research, 1985) p. 147, in Indian refugee camps for Tamils from Sri Lanka, "it was suggested to increase the dietary intake of Vitamin A to children between 1-6 years of age by supplying fish at subsidized rates to residents." One should be cautious because vitamin A is not available in high concentrations in fish flesh, and thus it may not provide sufficient quantities of the vitamin.

Chapter 4

USING FISH TO
ALLEVIATE MALNUTRITION

The contribution of fisheries to the alleviation of malnutrition can be enhanced through appropriate activities in the production, processing, and consumption phases of fisheries systems. Some actions which might be considered are suggested in the following sections.

PRODUCTION

Activities in the fishing industry may be distinguished into three major interacting phases: production (catching or culturing), processing, and marketing or other forms of distribution. In each phase there are things which could be done to help alleviate malnutrition.

Capture Fisheries

Fish production is generally targeted to those can best afford it and not to the poor. Fisheries development for the higher end of the market can even reduce the supplies available to the poor because productive resources are reallocated away from production for the poor.

To counteract these patterns, special measures are needed. One basic strategy is to support the production of low cost fish for consumption by the poor. This could be done by supporting fisheries--small-scale or large-scale, capture or culture--whose production is likely to

42

make a significant contribution to fish supplies used by the local poor. Or it could be done by supporting production by the poor themselves for their own consumption. Support could be in the form of technical assistance, infrastructure development, extension services, or subsidies. This support could be used to help develop specific fisheries at the same time it is used to respond to problems of malnutrition.

While supporting the production of low cost fish, policymakers should be alert to the geography of distribution. Where feasible, production should be supported directly in those regions in which malnutrition is most prevalent. It should be noted, also, that different types of fisheries tend to supply different markets. Small-scale fishing operations are likely to sell in the immediate vicinity while highly commercialized operations are more likely to market their catch in major urban markets or to export it. Where there are many small-scale operations there is a possibility that middlemen will buy and consolidate the catch and transport it to larger towns and cities. Thus it cannot be assumed that increasing production in a given area will necessarily mean increasing supplies available for consumption in that area.

Even if the product remains in the area, there is always the possibility that increasing supplies of fisheries products will go to the local middle class or local elite rather than to those most in need. For all these reasons, it would require expert knowledge of local fisheries, local markets, and local nutritional conditions to identify concrete situations in which this sort of strategy is likely to succeed.

It is generally preferable to have local production for local consumption in order to limit costs of processing and distribution and to help integrate local communities. Under some conditions, however, it may make sense to support production in one place in order to meet nutritional needs elsewhere. For example, underutilized fisheries resources in one part of the country might be developed in order to supply institutional feeding programs in other parts of the country.

Many seafoods other than finfish contribute to human nutrition, sometimes in small amounts for small numbers of people. Products such as seaweed,[1] clams, dugong, holuthurians, and various shellfish may have greater potential than would be suggested by their current limited patterns of use. Some, like iodine-rich seaweed, might be particularly valuable for dealing with specific nutrient deficiencies. In the Philippines and Thailand the mariculture of mussels is so highly productive that much of the product is wasted. It might be possible to find ways to use such products more effectively for alleviating local malnutrition.

Self-Provisioning

Many poor people have direct access to fish on coasts and in lakes, rivers, and irrigation ditches, and by fishing they can supplement their own and their families' diets. Pacific islands women spend a good deal of time gleaning on drying reefs and taking a harvest which, for them, is quite considerable. In some places such hunting continues to serve as an important source of animal protein long after hunting for land animals has become impractical. Some families have small ponds in which they culture fish for themselves, particularly in Southeast Asia. Since these are not commercial operations they have been almost wholly neglected by governments and by researchers.

At times the development of commercial fisheries has interfered with such "micro"-scale fishing. Yet these self-provisioning operations, which are quite different from what are commonly described as small-scale fisheries, can make a significant contribution to the alleviation of malnutrition. In seeking means for using fisheries products to alleviate malnutrition there may be a tendency to look to processed products (such as fish protein concentrate) which can be delivered through feeding programs. For the purpose of promoting human development, however, it is advisable to favor projects in which the poor can produce their own food, thus becoming active rather than passive participants in the process.

Self-provisioning might be tentatively defined as cases in which no more than half of one's production (capture or culture) is sold. The rest is either consumed or shared in some way. Sharing represents self-provisioning at the community level.

In some cases self-provisioning by the poor can be supported through improvements of fisheries resources in publicly accessible waters. Governments or other agencies could introduce fish through one-time transfers of species or they may undertake programs of regular stocking, repeatedly transferring fish into appropriate waters. They may also undertake other management measures such as fertilizing, feeding, and water control. Simple adaptations in the design of irrigation systems, for example, can greatly enhance their suitability for fish rearing.

According to one estimate, "Simply introducing the fish fry into a suitable environment--without induced feeding or substantial environmental changes--would make possible a modest production of 50 to 100 kilograms of fish per hectare per annum," and "Counting only natural lakes, coastal lagoons, and reservoirs of more than 50 hectares, Latin America has 10.5 million hectares in which such fish production can be carried out."[2]

Numerous lake and reservoir stocking projects have been undertaken in the Philippines and Thailand and other parts of Southeast Asia.[3] For example, on the island of Negros in the Philippines, where malnutrition is severe and widespread, the Augustinian sisters, working with the National Federation of Sugarworkers, imported freshwater snails and used them to stock streams near Bacolod City. The snails have no significant commercial value, but they are important in local self-provisioning. The government was not involved in this effort.

Stocking operations may be undertaken in wholly private waters or in wholly public waters, but there is also an intermediate possibility: stocking community-controlled waters. In Thailand, for example, the government helps to start and stock village fish ponds which are then managed by village committees.

More extensive stocking could be of great help in supporting self-provisioning by the poor, especially in remote areas. It might be useful to prepare a map of stockable waters and overlay this on a map showing areas of high poverty in order to estimate where the nutritional benefits of stocking are likely to be greatest.

In some areas it may be useful to support the construction of artificial reefs, fish aggregating devices, fish pens (for live storage), aquaculture operations, and solar driers based on the use of local materials with unpaid labor by local communities. In Ambon, Indonesia, for example, a private development organization, the Appropriate Mariculture Coordination Center (AMCOC) has assisted local people in building three artificial reefs out of used automobile tires, and it has also helped in building floating "brush parks" to provide new habitats for fish.

The major disadvantage of strategies to support self-provisioning is that there is no profit potential in it to provide motivation, and it may be resisted by commercial operators who fear their markets would decline if self-provisioning became widespread. The solution may be for government to focus on remote areas of great need where there is little ongoing commercial activity.

Aquaculture

Much of the excitement about modern aquaculture in the 1960s and 1970s was based on the idea that low-cost cultured fish or shellfish could make a significant contribution to alleviating malnutrition. Now, however, it is clear that commercial aquaculture operations are more responsive to the market demands of middle and upper classes, whether in domestic or export markets, for the simple reason that supplying people who have money generally is more profitable.

Moreover, modern aquaculture operations which use formulated feed can be net consumers rather than producers of protein. Feeds frequently contain substantial amounts of fish meal, which can mean that more fish is put in than is taken out. In many operations "the pond is actually consuming fish!"[4]

Just as market imperatives tend to lead to an increasing export orientation in capture fisheries, over time aquaculture is moving toward increasing export orientation. In several Southeast Asian countries traditional milkfish and shrimp polyculture ponds are being converted into monoculture shrimp ponds for the international market.[5] This trend increases the revenues to the owners of the ponds, but at the same time it may result in decreasing food supplies for local populations.

A clear distinction should be made between the modern, energy intensive, high technology methods for the culturing of fish which are currently drawing large capital investments as commercial ventures, and the traditional, centuries-old forms of aquaculture found in Southeast Asia, China, Egypt, and elsewhere. The modern form typically is a monoculture using high protein formulated feed, while traditional aquaculture is ordinarily a polyculture, using animal manure to stimulate algae growth, and often it is integrated with adjacent agriculture operations. While modern aquaculture operations generally yield high value products for the middle and upper classes, the products of traditional aquaculture normally are low value products destined for consumption at or near the production site. Thus, for the purpose of alleviating malnutrition, it may be more effective to strengthen traditional-style operations than to launch modern-style aquaculture operations.

The technological possibilities for culturing low cost products suitable for consumption by the poor are clear. Good prospects include tilapia, milkfish, carps, mussels and other species low on the food chain, with emphasis on fertilization of pond waters or using nutrients in naturally flowing waters rather than direct feeding.

Commercial aquaculture operations may be responsive to the poor if they are located in poor areas and have no easy access to "upscale" markets. They may be limited by their geographical distance to markets or they may be constrained by their modest capital and technology resources to focus only on products of interest to the local poor. The pattern is illustrated by the growth of tilapia culture in Jamaica.[6] Cultured fish also makes a significant contribution to the diet in Nepal. In the Philippines there is very widespread culturing of milkfish (*Chanos chanos*, or locally, *bangos*) which is favored by the poor. In Thailand village fish ponds have made a substantial contribution to meeting local nutritional needs, especially in the poor Northeast.[7]

PROCESSING

Fish may be processed for many different purposes, including preservation, maintaining quality control, making the product easier to transport, and making the product more attractive and palatable. The traditional, inexpensive means for processing or "curing" fish have been drying, smoking, salting, and fermenting, alone or in combinations. Other processed products such as the fish pastes used in Southeast Asia or the "fish glue" prepared in the household from common reef fish in some Pacific island communities, are less well known but also have comparable advantages. Traditionally processed fish products have very great advantages in that they involve low capital investments and low technological requirements, and they produce highly nutritious products of reduced perishability which are not only low in cost but are also readily accepted in many parts of the world.

Products of modern processing techniques include canned fish, fish protein concentrate, minced fish, and hydrolyzed fish. Although there are exceptions (such as Japanese canned mackerel), canning is generally regarded as suitable only for relatively expensive products. The production of fish protein concentrate, minced fish, and hydrolyzed fish are more suitable for producing large volumes of low cost products. These newer technologies for producing food for human consumption from fish are characterized by the fact that they transform the raw material into products that have lost their original identity as fish.

Fish Protein Concentrate

Fish protein concentrate is a stable protein supplement prepared from whole fish, usually fish of low market value. It is commonly prepared as a powder. The original form, now known as Type A, was vigorously promoted through the late 1960s and early 1970s as a response to the problem of malnutrition. It failed, however, partly because of the incorrect assumption that most malnutrition problems consisted simply of inadequate protein intake, partly because of inadequate attention to the food habits of local cultures, and partly because it was a high technology product intended for use under low technology circumstances.[8]

Interest now is focused on FPC Type B, which is fattier, smellier, has a stronger taste, and costs considerably less than Type A. While Type A was produced through a high technology process involving solvent extraction, the process for producing Type B is much simpler, similar to that for producing fish meal. It differs from fish meal production only in the fact that FPC-B production requires food grade fish and higher standards of quality control are exercised. In the late 1970s FPC-B cost about US$900 per ton, compared with dried skimmed milk (with roughly half the protein content) at about US$600 per ton.

Trials by the FAO Fisheries Department have indicated good acceptability of the product in food aid programs among populations accustomed to eating fish.[9] As a result the World Food Programme has made use of FPC-B in several countries. In Thailand the United Nations High Commissioner for Refugees has tried FPC-B among refugees from Vietnam, Laos, and Kampuchea. Some private voluntary organizations such as Catholic Relief Services have been using the product as well. In the Philippines, the Norwegian Mission Alliance Among Slum Dwellers in Manila has had good results with using FPC-B. In Sri Lanka FPC-B has been distributed through social (subsidized) marketing.[10]

Minced Fish

Minced (or pulped, or comminuted) fish is produced by the separation of bone, skin, viscera and scales from fish muscle with machines. The resulting raw material can be manufactured into a variety of different foods, including fish cakes, sticks, fingers, pastes, sausages, and burgers. The process appears to be very successful, but not for the purpose of alleviating malnutrition:

> . . . it is a technology that is booming in the developed nations to produce pre-cooked foods, portions for fast food eating places, additives for other foods, substitutes, and the like, all essentially designed for mass urban consumption in highly industrialized countries with well-developed and complex infrastructures. . . . the role of fish pulp in feeding lower income populations is still unclear, inasmuch as the use of fish pulp is, in fact, a form of putting fresh fish to use and is thus in competition with it.[11]

Thus minced fish has not yet been used to any great extent for the purpose of alleviating malnutrition.

Hydrolyzed Fish

Hydrolyzed fish is used as animal feed in the form of fish silage. Applications for human consumption are relatively new and untested. Fish protein hydrolysis is based on the splitting of the fibrous myocin into smaller units by enzymes of the fish itself or enzymes produced by microorganisms. The hydrolytic process liquefies fish muscle. The resulting product can be used in beverages (such as "leche de merluza"--hake milk), pharmaceutical products, institutional foods, and flavored dressings.[12] As a relatively new technology its use patterns are not yet well established.

There are a number of other low cost fisheries products which appear to have some potential for helping in the alleviation of malnutrition but which are not yet well established. For example, Iceland appears to have had good success with the production and marketing of fish pellets for direct human consumption, made largely from processing by-products. Similarly, it appears that roller dried fish might be useful, particularly in institutional feeding programs.[13]

50

By-Catch Utilization

A major source of raw material, helping to accelerate the developing of large-volume processing techniques, is by-catches, the fish caught incidentally during the catching of other more highly valued fish, especially in commercial fishing operations. The largest by-catches arise in trawling for shrimp, in which several tons of other species may be caught with each ton of shrimp that is taken. The by-catch may consist of commercially valuable species, as is often the case in Pacific Central America, or it may consist primarily of low-valued fish, as is usually the case in Southeast Asia. Low-value by-catches are generally described as "trash fish."

A distinction should be made between low value fish and low value species. Juveniles of some species are of low value, but would be of high value if allowed to mature.

In the past by-catches have been discarded, dumped back into the sea, because it was more economical for the catchers to save the available hold space for the more highly-valued species. In recent years, however, considerable effort has been made by national governments and international organizations to reduce the wastage represented by this dumping. One major use of the by-catch is the production of fishmeal, used primarily as feed for livestock.

The technology and marketing of fish meal has now become so highly developed and so demanding of raw material that fish suitable for direct human consumption is sometimes treated as if it were trash fish. Some large scale fishing operations are now specifically targeted on stocks intended for reduction to meal.[14]

Efforts also are being made to use more by-catch for direct human consumption. In Southeast Asia the Marine Fisheries Department of the Southeast Asian Fisheries Development Center (SEAFDEC), headquartered in Singapore, has processed by-catches to produce locally favored food items:

The leached mince in either the fresh or the frozen (surimi) form has been used by the Department for making a wide range of jelly products. In the Southeast Asian region, the most popular traditional fish-jelly products are fish balls and fishcakes. With the increase in price of raw materials used traditionally for these products, the fish-jelly product industry has to utilize other fish. The introduction of leached mince from by-catch and low market-value fish as a substitute raw material will provide impetus to the development of the industry in the region, as well as increasing the utilization of an abundant resource for human consumption.

The Department has successfully produced, on a pilot scale, fishballs and fish cakes from surimi made from by-catch. . . . Evaluation studies through trial sales at a local supermarket showed that the products were widely accepted by local consumers.[15]

As suggested by the practice of testing in supermarkets, most work on the improved use of by-catches is directed toward the regular commercial market. Only a part of the effort is geared specifically to producing low cost products for those most vulnerable to malnutrition.

DISTRIBUTION

Fisheries products intended to be used to help alleviate malnutrition can be distributed through conventional marketing, through "social marketing," or through institutional feeding programs. There is also the possibility of self-provisioning, where there is no distinct distribution phase.

Conventional Marketing

If the open market is to be used to promote the use of fish to alleviate malnutrition, attention should be centered on products consumed by the poor. The product should have a high price elasticity of demand among the poor and a low price elasticity of demand among middle and upper class consumers, since otherwise anything that is done to reduce fish prices would subsidize middle and upper classes as well.

Marketing should be attentive not only to prices but also to delivery mechanisms, to assure that poor communities have ready access to points of sale. Support services can be provided to vendors. In Southeast Asia street vendors play an especially important role in reaching the poor.

Government agencies responsible for fisheries and for nutrition could help representatives of the fishing industry undertake some aspects of this marketing. Their work could include marketing research and advertising among the poor and among the managers of relevant institutions. With some help from government, representatives of the industry might be willing to help sponsor and design specific programs such as nutrition education efforts.

Social Marketing

Social marketing is based on distribution through conventional marketing systems, but subsidies are introduced to assure lower than normal prices to consumers. Food stamp programs, for example, are mechanisms for social marketing. The Nutripak in the Philippines has been distributed through social marketing. Experiments have been undertaken in the Philippines on the effectiveness of discounting the prices of rice and cooking oil in selected nutritionally depressed areas.

A social marketing scheme specifically devoted to fish was established in Egypt in 1964. The Egyptian Fish Marketing Company operated an extensive distribution system devoted specifically to supplying poorer customers.

Institutional Feeding

Institutional feeding programs include all programs in which the delivery of food to consumers is organized by persons other than the consumers themselves. Such feeding programs may be found in schools, prisons, hospitals, factories, and many other contexts. The term also includes direct feeding programs designed specifically to alleviate malnutrition. These may take the form of congregate dining arrangements, take-home meals, or home-delivered meals. The common characteristic of these programs of interest here is the fact that decisions regarding the choice of foods are made by a manager rather than by the final consumers, and that the manager's criteria are likely to be significantly different from the consumers'. In all of these cases the manager is likely to be acutely cost conscious, and--particularly in the case of direct feeding programs--the manager is likely to be more concerned with the nutritional quality of the products than the average consumer. Although feeding programs are non-market operations from the point of view of consumers, often the managers of such programs must purchase their foods on the open market. Thus these managers should be included in marketing efforts.

Institutional feeding programs are of particular interest because they offer the possibility of using fisheries products to alleviate malnutrition on terms that are commercially attractive. As the chief of the fishery and forestry section of the Inter-American Development Bank points out:

> . . . the institutional demand for foodstuffs (where the selection of the product and its form of preparation does not directly depend on the consumer but on an institutional center) may create favorable conditions for establishing a large market. It should be borne in mind that by itself the school food program in Brazil provides 25 million daily rations, while in Peru and Chile hundreds of thousands of tons of good quality fish are used to produce meal for animal consumption because of the lack of a

commercial option in the human consumption market.[16]

The school lunch program in Brazil uses large quantities of FPC-A produced in the country from local sardines.[17]

Of the many different possible institutional outlets (such as schools, industrial lunch programs, hospitals, prisons, and the military), if the focus is to be on alleviating malnutrition, the single most suitable objective is likely to be school feeding programs since children are particularly vulnerable to malnutrition. Moreover school lunch programs are likely to be very centrally organized, and thus can be accessed readily. Day care centers for pre-school children also may provide a good opportunity.

It is advantageous to have school feeding programs coordinated with nutrition assessment programs. Recording students' heights, weights, and ages can be of great help in assessing the impacts of feeding programs.

In some areas the more serious cases of malnutrition are to be found among children who do not attend school. Those children should be reached in some way. However, even if the most extreme cases are not in the schools, it may be worthwhile to establish or strengthen school feeding programs for several different reasons. Even if only a few students in school are seriously malnourished, the school can be a good channel through which they can be reached. Larger numbers of students may be mildly malnourished and might benefit from supplemental feeding. Schools may be able to feed children more readily and more cheaply than they could be fed at home; thus school feeding programs can be viewed as a means for helping the family as a whole. Fishery products in school lunches may be used simply to diversify the diet, or to replace a lower quality protein source. The use of novel food products of high nutritive value (such as FPC) in the schools may help to build acceptance in the community as a whole. Finally, beyond the immediate nutritional considerations, the regular use of fishery products in school feeding can help in the development of the local fishing industry.

Commercial operations are most responsive to the middle and upper classes because they have the money to create a market demand. However, selling uniform products in large numbers for institutional feeding programs can be a profitable way to be responsive to the needs of the poor. Such programs are commercially attractive because of the consolidation of demand in a single decision-making manager, resulting in potentially large economies of scale. The fact that school lunch programs often are subsidized adds to their commercial attractiveness.

Fish in International Aid

Just as fish can be used in nutrition intervention programs within countries, it can be used in international food assistance programs. Fish protein concentrate, dried fish, and canned fish have been used for this purpose. The World Food Programme used between 9,000 and 13,000 metric tons of fish per year in its food aid programs from 1980 to 1983. In each year, between 6,500 and 8,500 metric tons of this has been comprised of canned fish. The major donors have been Canada, Germany, the Netherlands, and Norway, with Norway the largest contributor of fish products to WFP. Some 70 countries have received these products, half of them in Africa. However, fish products comprise less than one percent of the food used by WFP.[18]

Apparently WFP regards fish products as expensive ($1500-$3,000 per metric ton compared to $280 for dried skimmed milk powder and $500 for pulses), but fish products might compare favorably when assessed on the basis of nutritional value.

Some commodities used in international food aid programs, such as Norway's Norse Fish Powder, are produced in developed countries. WFP recognizes that extra benefits could be provided for developing countries if the fisheries products that are used in aid programs were obtained from less developed countries, and thus help to develop their fisheries. The products might be obtained from the country that is to receive the products or from other less developed countries, possibly in the same region. Guaranteed purchases of this sort could help to make marginal fishing operations commercially viable, and they could help to assure that fish that otherwise would be diverted to animal feed is used for direct human consumption. Since 1980 about 19,000 tons of dried and canned fish, valued at over US$23 million, have been bought in Thailand on behalf of bilateral donors, UNHCR, and UNICEF for the Kampuchean emergency operation.[19] In the Philippines, aid programs could draw from the relatively underutilized fishery resources of Palawan. Even if the product were used elsewhere, increased incomes could result in improved nutrition on Palawan itself.

Spinoff Nutrition

Industrialized fisheries may sometimes reduce the fish supplies available to local people in less developed countries because of their export orientation, but at times they may improve local supplies. In Majuro in the Marshall Islands, for example, foreign purse seiners sometimes offer small or damaged tunas to local people. The Japanese-owned tuna cannery at Taguig, Metro-Manila in the Philippines sells heads and tails to street vendors who sell them to the local poor for use in their cooking. (They are considerably cheaper than the popular milkfish or *galonggong* on a unit weight basis; it is not clear how they would compare in terms of cost in relation to nutritive value.)[20]

The joint venture tuna cannery in Solomon Islands ships most of the prime quality pack off to Europe, but it sells the lower grade canned tuna flakes locally. One might object to the fact that so much high quality food is being shipped away from a poor country, but that tuna might never have become available to the local people in the absence of the joint venture. Thus, while it is true that the cannery represents a negative "nutritional balance of trade," the canned tuna flakes that are retained may actually represent a net nutritional gain.

In some cases canneries intended to provide fish for the local community can be made economically viable only by exporting some portion of the pack.

In India and elsewhere, shark fisheries are motivated by the lucrative Japanese market for shark fins, but they also produce good quantities of low cost shark meat.

Spinoff effects can take place in aquaculture operations. With appropriate design, culturing operations geared to an "upscale" commercial market can also produce low cost products for the poor at little incremental cost, little enough to make the added line profitable. The commercial product may justify and absorb much of the cost of operations and thus in effect subsidize the product of the "downscale" products.

This practice is widespread in Southeast Asia, where milkfish for local consumption is raised along with shrimp for export. An experiment is being undertaken at the Brackishwater Aquaculture Center in the Philippines on culturing sea bass together with tilapia. The high value sea bass feed on the small tilapia, while the larger tilapia can be sold cheaply for human consumption. Raising the two species together results in improved production of both.

Backyard aquaculture operations useful for self-provisioning may be more feasible economically if some portion of the product could be sold locally for cash.

Another possible source of spinoff nutrition is by-catches, particularly from shrimp trawling operations. Some of the by-catch is discarded at sea and some is processed into meal, but some may be used for direct consumption. Extensive research is underway in the Philippines, Thailand and elsewhere on the use of by-catch in FPC or other directly consumed products. In El Salvador the by-catch is used without processing of any kind. Shrimp trawlers sometimes give away their by-catches, filling the dugout canoes of locals fishers--who then sell the "catch" on shore for low prices.

Low cost products may be left behind by commercial operations more or less accidentally, but the phenomenon suggests some opportunities for deliberate policymaking. Just as homebuilders or automakers are sometimes required by government to provide some low cost products in return for the privilege of working at the high end of the socioeconomic spectrum, so fish producers and processors might be required to provide some amount of low cost product for the local community. This could become an element in joint venture or access negotiations. While local people might just naturally benefit from by-products of commercial operations, uncertainties could be resolved by insisting that such products must be made available on favorable terms if such commercial operations are to be permitted.

The idea in spinoff nutrition is that in some circumstances food for the poor can be produced as a by-product of processes which serve the middle and higher segments of the market. For some this might be objectionable as a matter of principle because it rationalizes providing cake for the rich on the grounds that it yields crumbs for the poor. Nevertheless, it sometimes provides practical opportunities which should not be ignored.

Nutrition Education

Both poverty and ignorance contribute to malnutrition. With meager resources people have few alternatives, and with meager information people do not choose well among the alternatives that they do have. Nutrition education programs are of very little use to the absolute poor who have hardly any choices to make. However such programs may make a considerable difference for those who do have some resources to allocate.

Generalized educational programs about the nutritive qualities of fish are not likely to be very effective in helping to alleviate malnutrition, particularly in Southeast Asia where most people already have a good appreciation of fish. However, carefully targeted practical programs may be of value. Educational programs could focus on methods of self-provisioning through fishing, and on methods of preparing and preserving fish, with emphasis placed on inexpensive and readily accessible species.

Rather than creating new programs specifically to deal with fish, it may be better to give attention to fish in broader nutrition education programs. In the Philippines, for example, a series of radio broadcasts encouraged mothers to add fish to their babies' lugaw (rice porridge) and to give fish to children at the evening meal.[21]

Nutrition education programs organized by nutrition agencies can draw on fisheries specialists to provide information regarding the fisheries components of the program.

NOTES

1. Charlotte Bruce, "Seaweed as Food," *INFOFISH Marketing Digest*, No. 4/83 (July-August 1983), pp. 27-29.
2. Julio Luna, "Fishery Resources," *Natural Resources in Latin America* (Washington, D.C.: Inter-American Development Bank, 1983) p. 80.
3. Elvira A. Baluyut, *Stocking and Introduction of Fish in Lakes and Reservoirs in the ASEAN (Association of Southeast Asian Nations) Countries*, FAO Fisheries Technical Paper 236 (Rome: Food and Agriculture Organization of the United Nations, 1983). According to Baluyut (p. 76), in 1979 in the Philippines, Laguna de Bay yielded 250kg/ha/year, and Lake Baluan yielded 1600 kg/ha/year, figures far higher than Luna's estimates. However, most of this "stocking" was in privately-owned cages and pens, and thus might be better described as aquaculture. Attempts to raise fish with rice have not been very successful, partly because of the increasing use of pesticides in rice growing areas. H. R. Rabanal, "Aquaculture in Asia and the Pacific," *INFOFISH Marketing Digest*, No. 1/83 (January/February 1983), pp. 16-18.
4. Barry A. Pierce, *Ecological Studies of Semi-Intensive Prawn Aquaculture Ponds* (Honolulu: Doctoral

60

Dissertation in Oceanography, University of Hawaii, 1984), p. 9.

5. Richard A. Neal and Ian R. Smith, "Key Problems in World Aquaculture Development," *ICLARM Newsletter*, Vol. 3 (1982), pp. 3-5.

6. T. J. Popma, F. E. Ross, B. L. Nerrie, and J. R. Bowman, *The Development of Commercial Farming of Tilapia in Jamaica 1979-1983* (Auburn University, Alabama: Alabama Agricultural Experiment Station, 1984).

7. George Kent, "Aquaculture: Motivating Production for Low-Income Markets," and "Sharing the Catch at Village Level: Fish-Ponds in Thailand," *Ceres: FAO Review on Agriculture and Development*, Vol. 19, No. 4 (July-August 1986), pp. 23-27; Catharina van Heel, "Village Fishponds in Thailand," *Food and Nutrition*, Vol. 12, No. 2 (1986), pp. 44-47.

8. E. R. Pariser et al., *Fish Protein Concentrate: Panacea for Protein Malnutrition?"* (Cambridge, Massachusetts: MIT Press, 1978). Moreover, there was considerable resistance to its approval by some elements of the dairy industry. See Edward Wenk, Jr., *The Politics of the Ocean* (Seattle: University of Washington Press, 1972), pp. 312-319.

9. Maria A. Tagle, S. Valand, and D. B. James, "Acceptability Testing of FPC Type B in Selected Developing Areas," in *Proceedings of the Conference on Handling, Processing, and Marketing of Tropical Fish* (London: Tropical Products Institute, 1977), pp. 261-268.

10. S. Valand, "Fish Protein Concentrate Type B--A More Promising Approach," *Food and Nutrition*, Vol. 5, No. 2 (1979), pp. 24-30.

11. Julio Luna (ed.), *Non-Traditional Fish Products for Massive Human Consumption* (Washington, D.C.: Inter-American Development Bank, 1981), pp. 35-37.

12. Luna (ed.), *Non-Traditional Fish Products for Massive Human Consumption*.

13. Lars Herborg, *The Feasibility of Producing Roller Dried Fish in Thailand* (Rome: FAO Consultancy Report, 1983).

14. A paradoxical inversion of the by-catch problem can result. In the North Sea, fishing operators pursuing fish for reduction can be fined if they take fish suitable for direct human consumption. Thus this by-catch of high-value fish is sometimes discarded at sea.
15. Tan Sen Min, Tatsuru Fujiwara, Ng Mui Chng, and Tan Ching Ean, "Processing of By-Catch into Frozen Minced Blocks (Surimi) and Jelly Products," *Fish By-Catch . . . Bonus from the Sea*, p. 90.
16. Julio Luna, "Fishery Resources," *Natural Resources in Latin America* (Washington, D.C.: Inter-American Development Bank, 1983), pp. 87-88. Also see Julio Luna, "A New Type of Bank to Eliminate Hunger," *ITCC Review*, Vol. 4, No. 44 (1982), pp. 36-38.
17. E. R. Pariser and E. Ruckes, *Non-Traditional Foods from Fish for Institutional Markets (Ecuador-Peru-Chile-Brazil)* (Washington, D.C.: Inter-American Development Bank, 1983).
18. The contribution of fishery products by Norway and Sweden are described in Group for International Nutrition, Institute for Nutrition Research, *Nordic Food Aid: Problems and Policy Issues in an International Development Perspective* (Oslo: Nordic Council of Ministers' Secretariat, 1980).
19. World Food Programme, *World Food Programme Assistance for Fisheries Development in Third World Countries and the Use of Fish Products in Food Aid* (Rome: WFP, 1984), pp. 11-12.
20. The prices of spinoff products may not be as low as they seem. In 1972 local people in Palau, in Micronesia, were allowed to buy skipjack that was too small for canning for US$0.12 per pound. This amounted to US$264 per metric ton, considerably higher than the US$150 then being obtained for fish suitable for canning.
21. Marian F. Zeitlin and Candelaria S. Formacion, *Nutrition Intervention in Developing Countries: Study II, Nutrition Education* (Cambridge, Massachusetts: Oelgeschlager, Gunn & Hain, 1981), pp. 228-241.

PART 2

NATIONAL AND REGIONAL CASE STUDIES

Chapter 5

THE PHILIPPINES

NUTRITION

Nutrition has been a major national concern in the Philippines since soon after World War II when the Philippine Association of Nutrition was founded.[1] In 1974 the Philippine Nutrition Program launched Operation Timbang to systematically identify malnourished children. Over four million children 0 to 6 years old in selected depressed areas were weighed, and it was found that only 21 percent of these children were adequately fed. Thus it became clear that there was a need to assess a national sample of the population.

The first nationwide nutrition survey was conducted in 1978 by the Food and Nutrition Research Institute of the National Science Development Board. The study showed that less than half the children surveyed had normal weights for their ages. Over 20 percent of the children were moderately or severely malnourished. Serious protein deficiencies were found among second and third degree malnourished children and in pregnant women and lactating mothers. Anemia was also prevalent among pregnant and lactating women.[2]

A review by the World Bank indicated widespread malnutrition in the Philippines. Overall calorie intake averaged only 87 percent of the Recommended Dietary Allowance (RDA). Consumption of fish, meat and poultry together, at a total of 48.5 kg/capita, was estimated to be at 85.5 percent of sufficiency. Vitamin A intake averaged only 67 percent of RDA. In Mindanao and the Visayas fat intake was estimated as being only a quarter of sufficiency. The data showed a very clear inverse correlation between income levels and intake levels of all major nutrients.[3] The government issued a *Food and Nutrition Plan* in 1980.[4] The aim of the program is to raise average per capita energy consumption to 2,030 calories per day by the year 1990, and in particular to improve the consumption levels of the lowest income group. While several different kinds of direct intervention programs are to be used, emphasis is being placed on increasing the production of food and assuring that food prices remain at reasonable levels.

A second nationwide nutrition survey was conducted in 1982 by the Food and Nutrition Research Institute. In comparison with the 1978 survey, the 1982 survey showed a 4.8 percent reduction in the proportion of households whose energy level was below 80 percent of adequacy. There was a 7.2 percent decrease in the proportion of the households with protein adequacy below 70 percent of adequacy. In 1982 average energy intake was 1808 kilocalories per person, for 89 percent of adequacy, and average protein intake was 50.6 grams per person, for 99.6 percent of adequacy. The 1982 survey showed modest improvements in many categories, but at the same time it showed that the problems identified in 1978 were still very serious.[5]

The National Nutrition Council, which formulates the *Food and Nutrition Plan*, is the nation's principal policy-making and coordinating body in nutrition. It formulated the framework for the plan for 1983-87, which "represents the initial attempt of the Philippine Government to operationalize the strategy of integrating nutrition objectives in development plans and programs."[6] Under the guidance of the National Nutrition Council, the Philippine Nutrition Program coordinates all food assistance programs.

Inexpensive fish products have been used in some supplemental feeding programs. One example is the Nutripak program developed by the Nutrition Center of the Philippines, a private organization:

The Nutripak consists of three separate plastic pouches, containing correct proportions of broken rice, oil, and a cheap minifish, mini-shrimp, or bean-protein supplement, which are enclosed with cooking instructions in a larger plastic bag. Nutripaks are produced in three sizes that differ slightly in composition for three different preschool age ranges, and are designed to provide half of the daily calorie and protein requirements of the six-month to six-year old child. Mothers of third-degree malnourished children are supplied free Nutripaks daily for six weeks and are taught how to prepare the Nutripak in a group cooking lesson.[7]

As of 1981 the World Food Programme had provided to the Philippines a total assistance of US$33.8 million for 30 development projects and seven emergency operations. In one example, soy-fortified wheat flour or corn-soy meal was baked into "nutribuns" for approximately 500,000 elementary school children in Mindanao between 1977 and 1980. In another case, a program was undertaken to supplement the diets of preschool children on Mindanao using contributed corn-soya milk and dried skim milk enriched with vitamin A, in 1980-1983.

FISHERIES

In 1974-1976 fish accounted for 22.6 percent of total protein supplies in the Philippines, a level second only to that of Japan.[8] "Fish is the main and cheapest source of animal protein. Per capita consumption of fresh fish for 1978-1980 was placed at 30 kg (66 lb.) or 62 percent of animal protein intake."[9] Fish prices have been relatively low in comparison with meat, poultry, and dairy products.

Presidential Decree 704 of 1975 emphasized achievement of "the maximum economic utilization" of the Philippines' fishery resources. As a result the nation's fisheries development became largely export oriented. The economic benefits have been considerable, but at the same time there has been a reduced supply of fish for local consumption:

Until quite recently the Philippines was a net importer of fish, primarily canned mackerel and sardines from Japan. Imports augmented local production which in part led to increasing domestic per capita supply in the first half of the 1970s. As a result of the imposition of import quotas on canned fish in 1976 and the tremendous growth of tuna exports, the Philippines became a net exporter of edible fish products. Consequently, supply for local consumption declined from its highest level of 25.9 kilograms per capita in 1976 to 22.9 kilograms per capita in 1980, the same level of supply as in 1970.[10]

Numerous surveys have confirmed that consumption of fish products of all types (except canned fish) has been declining. Government policy calls for full exploitation of the country's fisheries resources with the intention of maintaining self-sufficiency in fish supply, improving handling and distribution, strengthening small-scale fisheries, and increasing the earnings of foreign exchange from exports. The *Food and Nutrition Plan* calls for improvement in fish marketing, the development of small-scale fishponds, improving the living conditions of small-scale fishermen, and strengthening the culturing of fish in rice fields through the Palay-Isdaan program.[11] The national development plan for 1983-87 says that "self-sufficiency in fish will be maintained to satisfy the protein requirements of the population.[12]

ACTION PROGRAM

In the mid-1980s the Philippines planned an integrated program of pilot projects to implement, at the national level, the FAO "Action Programme on the Promotion of the Role of Fisheries in Alleviating Undernutrition" which was approved in Rome in July 1984.
Five specific lines of action were considered:

1. *Aquaculture Village.* Staff members of UP-V have drawn up plans for an integrated

agriculture/aquaculture operation, based on brackishwater aquaculture. The proposed aquaculture village would be organized as an entirely new community, with about fifteen selected families. Emphasis would be placed on food production both for the village itself and for the surrounding community.

2. *Tilapia in Elementary Schools.* Tilapia ponds in elementary schools can provide much-needed protein for school lunches, and they can also be used as teaching instruments, both for the students and for their parents. Some school ponds have been established in the Philippines, but their usefulness needs to be carefully assessed and their operations need to be strengthened.

3. *Stocking Public Waters.* Stocking publicly accessible waters can be a significant means of providing fish supplies to the poor, especially in inland areas. Where it is feasible in biological terms, suitable waters will be stocked, and the impact on local nutrition will be systematically assessed.

4. *Nutrition and the Role of Women in Fishing Villages.* The fishing village of Kirayan is the subject of an extensive social science research program already underway. Specific elements would be added to that study to focus on nutrition and the role of women. One question of interest is the relationship between the work patterns of women and the nutritional status of their children.

5. *FPC Acceptability in Schools.* Fish protein concentrate can be a good source of high quality protein in school lunch programs. The acceptability of FPC in different recipes would be investigated.

Several other possibilities were also considered:

* The Nutripak used in feeding programs in many areas of the Philippines currently uses a corn-soy meal mix for its protein component. It might be less costly to use some form of fisheries product, possibly from nearby Palawan where there are considerable underutilized fisheries resources.

* Mussels can be produced cheaply in very large quantities. Current research into the possibilities for processing mussel meat (beyond simple drying), perhaps for use in institutional feeding programs, could be accelerated.

* Small aquaculture operations in the Philippines appear to have good local nutritional effects. Research work already done on their economic impact could be augmented with research to assess their nutritional impacts, possibly through joint activities involving the National Nutrition Council, the Food and Nutrition Research Institute, ICLARM, and fisheries and nutrition research centers in the university system.

* The Food and Nutrition Institute could investigate the usefulness of FPC-B and other fisheries products as weaning foods.

* As part of the National Nutrition Program, the Bureau of Fisheries and Aquatic Resources offers courses on the utilization of fisheries products to housewives, teachers, and extension workers. On the basis of this substantial experience, training manuals could be prepared to support further extension of such teaching programs.

* Trial use of suitable fishery products could be undertaken in institutional settings. For example, in accordance with the Philippine Nutrition Program Implementing Guidelines on Food Assistance, trials might be undertaken with inexpensive, simply

prepared tilapia in nutritionally depressed areas under the guidance of the National Nutrition Council.

The University of the Philippines, Visayas, in the city of Iloilo has been designated to specialize in fisheries. Thus it can serve as an institutional base for the Philippine program on the use of fisheries in alleviating malnutrition. The program that was planned was to be conducted by UP-V together with the Regional Technical Group for Nutrition (comprised of regional representatives of each of the concerned government agencies) and with appropriate governmental and other agencies in Manila. However, the effort was disrupted by the change of government in February 1986. The opportunities for using fisheries to help alleviate malnutrition in the Philippines remain very substantial.

NOTES

1. Conrad R. Pascual, "Nutrition in the Philippines," in Donald S. McLaren, ed., *Nutrition in the Community* (New York: Wiley, 1976), pp. 345-355.
2. Food and Nutrition Institute, National Science Board, *First Nationwide Nutrition Survey, Philippines, 1978 (Summary Report)* (Manila: FNI, NSB, 1979).
3. World Bank, *Aspects of Poverty in the Philippines: A Review and Assessment* (Washington, D.C.: WB, 1980); Philip Bowring, "The Poverty Puzzle," *Far Eastern Economic Review*, March 27, 1981, pp. 125-131.
4. National Nutrition Council, *Food Policy and Nutrition Plan* (Manila: NNC, 1980).
5. Gracia M. Villavieja et al., *Second Nationwide Nutrition Survey: Philippines, 1982*, presented at First National Nutrition Congress, July 1984.

6. *National Nutrition Council: Annual Report 1982* (Manila: NNC, 1982), p 4.

7. Marian F. Zeitlin and Candelaria S. Formacion, *Nutrition Intervention in Developing Countries: Study II, Nutrition Education* (Cambridge, Massachusetts: Oelgeschlager, Gunn & Hain, 1981), p. 85. Also see "Formulated Foods in the Philippines: Nutripak," in James E. Austin, *Nutrition Programs in the Third World: Cases and Readings* (Cambridge: Massachusetts: Oelgeschlager, Gunn & Hain, 1981), pp. 176-200.

8. Helga Josupeit, *The Economic and Social Effects of the Fishing Industry: A Comparative Study* (Rome: Food and Agriculture Organization of the United Nations, 1981), p. 3.

9. Elizabeth D. Samson, "Fisheries," in George Kent and Mark J. Valencia, eds., *Marine Policy in Southeast Asia* (Berkeley: University of California Press, 1984).

10. Jesse M. Floyd, *The Role of Fish in Nutrition in Four Selected Countries of Southeast Asia.* Consultant's report to the Food Policy and Nutrition Division, FAO, 1984, pp. 55-57.

11. *The Food and Nutrition Plan (Objectives and Strategies)* (Manila: Republic of the Philippines, 1980), p. 9.

12. *National Economic and Development Authority, Five-Year Philippine Development Plan, 1983-1987: Technical Annex* (Manila: NEDA, 1982), p. 50.

Chapter 6

THAILAND

NUTRITION

Despite its vigorous economy, Thailand has widespread protein-energy malnutrition. In a survey of one million children under five conducted in 1980-81, 35 percent were mildly malnourished, 13 percent were moderately malnourished, and 2 percent were severely malnourished. In a sample of schoolchildren from the Northern region, 22 percent were found to be deficient in iodine. In the rural population, 43 percent of the females and 29 percent of the males were found to be deficient in iron.[1]

Nutrition policy is the primary responsibility of the Ministry of Public Health through the National Food and Nutrition Committee. Formed in 1970, the committee is comprised of the Permanent Secretaries of the concerned ministries (primarily Public Health, Agriculture and Cooperatives, Education, and Interior) and the Secretary General of the National Economic and Social Development Board (NESDB), and is chaired by the Minister of Public Health. It formulates policies, programs, and projects for submission to the NESDB for integration into the National Development Policy.

The *Fifth National Economic and Social Development Plan (1982-1986)* sets a variety of policies regarding the alleviation of malnutrition.[2] It emphasizes the problems of specific groups, particularly pregnant and lactating mothers, and children, especially in rural areas. The strategy concentrates on primary health care organized through tambon councils. The plan acknowledges that the

73

rural poor face serious problems of malnutrition "because the staple diet of fish is fast disappearing."[3]

The fifth five-year plan supports the development of food self-sufficiency in poor provinces, and does not encourage the inflow of foods for nutrition intervention programs. The activity projects include Village Fish Ponds and Village Fisheries, both to be implemented by the Department of Fisheries.

It is intended that by the end of the decade school lunch programs will be based on the students' own production of food. However, in January 1983 the Subcommittee on Food Production and Distribution submitted a report to the National Committee on Food and Nutrition suggesting that a feasibility study on supplementary feeding should be carried out.[4]

Thailand has shown very great interest in processed foods. The Institute for Food Research and Product Development (IFRPD) at Kasetsart University has developed many different varieties of Kaset Protein. These were based on mung bean or soybean protein, but also included fish protein concentrate and a fish sauce based on mussels. The FPC has been imported. Attempts to use the product in school lunch programs have encountered many obstacles, the most important of which was the inability of many students to pay the price of about nine cents for the lunch.[5]

Apart from the nutrition programs undertaken by the Thai government for Thai nationals, there are programs for refugees in camps and holding centers. These involve outside agencies such as the World Food Programme (WFP), the Committee for American Relief Everywhere (CARE), and the United Nations High Commissioner for Refugees (UNHCR). WFP is a major purchaser of locally produced foods for these programs. Monthly purchases have included some 200 tons of dried and salted fish, mostly mackerel, and 150 tons of canned fish. The dried salted fish is purchased for around 8 to 12 baht per kilogram, and the canned fish is bought for about 17 to 18 baht per kilogram.[6]

FISHERIES

In Thailand fish accounts for about half of the animal protein and 14 percent of the total protein consumed. Following a period of rapid growth in fisheries production through the 1960s and early 1970s, production peaked in 1977 and has slowed since then. As a result of overcapitalization in trawlers and other gear in the boom years and the overfishing which followed, the catch per unit of fishing effort has declined, and much more of the catch is comprised of low value species. In 1980 trash fish landings (used for fishmeal and fertilizer) comprised over 40 percent of total production of marine fish.

The strong export orientation of the Thai fishing industry has limited the supplies available for domestic consumption:

> In spite of declining production since 1977 and the increasing volume of trash fish landings, fish product exports have continued to expand because of favorable export prices. Between 1970 and 1979 marine product exports grew at an average annual rate of 22 percent by volume and 40 percent by value, reaching their highest level in 1981 of 305,000 mt valued at US$403.8 million. Approximately 40 percent of export production since 1977 has been fishmeal and fertilizer. The remainder has been edible fish products popular on domestic markets . . . .[7]

High export levels, low import levels, declining overall production, increasing trash fish production, and increasing population have combined to reduce available per capita fish supplies. In the early 1970s the supply was over 25 kilograms per capita, but the level reduced to 13.1 kilograms in 1980 and 15.2 kilograms in 1981.[8]

About a third of the by-catch from trawl fisheries consists of species which could be used for direct human consumption if allowed to mature. One observer suggests that "the predominance of trash fish (and indeed the depletion of the resource) is explained by the fact that trawlers fish for shrimp using small mesh nets that catch juveniles of other species and inhibit the growth of adult fish.[9] Moreover, some of what is considered as trash fish in Thailand would be used directly as food fish in other countries.

The limitation of supplies available for domestic production has created considerable upward pressure on domestic fish prices. The average real price of fish has increased around 15 percent annually since 1976.

To counteract these trends the government of Thailand has been encouraging the development of aquaculture and is promoting the development of processing technologies to allow increased use of fish by-catches for direct human consumption. Much of the research work on processing is being undertaken in the Fishery Technological Development Division of the Department of Fisheries. The division has been experimenting with fish crackers, fish noodles, fish biscuits, fish-protein concentrate, dried minced fish, and canned goods, and has given particular attention to *lukchin pla*, fish balls. There are some 40 fish ball factories in Bangkok alone which could make good use of more inexpensive raw materials.

Research is also being undertaken at the Institute of Food Research and Product Development of Kasetsart University. With the support of FAO the institute has been investigating the possibility of incorporating fish protein concentrate and roller dried fish into traditional Thai dishes.[10]

ACTION PROGRAM

The government of Thailand formulated a program on the use of fisheries products for alleviating malnutrition as part of its preparation for the *Sixth National Economic and Social Development Plan*. The program is coordinated by the Department of Fisheries under the Ministry of Agriculture and Cooperatives. At the outset, seven major project areas were considered:

1. *Supplemental Feeding Packets.* Supplemental feeding packets are now being used in programs organized by the Institute of Nutrition

of Mahidol University, and in Bangkok in programs of the Bangkok Metropolitan Authority. The protein component of these packets is based on soybeans or mung beans. Trials on the use of fisheries products in these packets would be useful, giving attention not only to protein needs but also to needs for vitamin A, iodine, and iron.

2. *Fish Ponds.* Both the government and the Population and Community Development Association (a non-governmental development organization) have launched extensive programs of pond development. (UNICEF also has a pond program.) Systematic assessments may be made of the disposition of the catches and of their nutritional impacts on local communities. The innovative schemes for community management of village ponds may be documented to make this information available to other countries. Manuals and teaching materials may be prepared on starting, using, and teaching with school fish ponds.

3. *Urban Poor.* The patterns of use of fishery products in the Bangkok slums will be examined, giving special consideration to marketing systems, pricing, and quality control. Programs may then be devised for improving the availability of fish for the urban poor.

4. *Institutional Feeding.* Extended trials may be undertaken on the use of fishery products in schools and other institutional settings. The Institute of Food Research and Product Development might take primary responsibility for the selection or formulation of the product and for laboratory testing, the Department of Education might take primary responsibility for coordinating its use in the schools, and the Institute of Nutrition might design the field study of the suitability of the product.

Particular consideration might be given to the usefulness of FPC-B and of institutional-pack canned fish.

5. *Economics of Improved Utilization.* Much of the fish caught in Thailand is wasted and much of the fish that could be used for direct human consumption is used instead as fish meal for livestock feed. Utilization needs to be improved both in economic terms and in nutritional terms--and these two do not always correspond. Careful attention must be paid not only to the techniques but also to the adequacy of incentives for improvements in utilization.

6. *Education and Training.* There is room for improvement in preservation, preparation, and quality control in fish handling, both by consumers and by the industry. Suitable teaching materials and formats will need to be developed.

7. *Nutrition Status of Fishworkers.* Workers in the fishing industry--men, women, and children working in the production, processing, and marketing phases of the industry--often are among the most malnourished groups, despite the fact that they are food producers. This needs to be studied to determine the extent to which it is a problem and to find ways to remedy it. Distinctions would have to be made among different types of workers, such as the self-employed in fishing villages, sub-contractors, and salaried workers in industrial processing plants. These issues can be studied in existing fishing operations, or they may be studied in inland villages which are just now moving into large-scale aquaculture operations.

The government has emphasized the village fish pond program, which was launched in 1982 and accounts for almost a fifth of the Department of Fisheries' budget.

Under the program poor villages can request the Department of Fisheries to prepare and seed ponds for them. The ponds are then managed by village committees. The government funds the pond projects completely in the first year, 50 percent in the second year, and 25 percent in the third year. Thereafter the government provides only advisory services. By the end of 1986 about 500 ponds were established, averaging about 100 new ponds per year over the Fifth Plan period.

Some ponds operate on the basis of selling licenses to fish on the designated fishing days. There has been some concern that those who need it most might be deterred from fishing by the license fees. Other ponds operate differently. For example, in the Buan Hua Chang pond near Ban Thad village in Surin Province, which was started in 1983, the village committee itself does the fishing. Committee members who participate in the fishing operations each get a free lunch and about two kilograms of fish. Membership on the committee changes every two years by an election process.

In contrast with some village fish ponds which have only one or two fishing days each year, the Buan Hua Chang pond is harvested about once a week, with harvests totaling about 100 kilograms. Most of the fish is sold and consumed in the six member villages, but perhaps 10 percent of it is traded, often for rice. In some ponds most of the catch is sold to outsiders, which means that there is little direct nutritional benefit from the fish.

In the mid-1980s individuals from the six member villages could buy the fish at 15 baht per kilogram, while outsiders could buy fish at 20 baht per kilogram. Comparable fish at the regular market sold for well over 20 baht per kilogram. Sales from the pond were limited to about five kilograms per person to assure wide distribution and to reduce the likelihood that the fish would be sold rather than being consumed in the family.

The villages rather than the committee decide how the earnings from license fees and sales are to be used. About 30 percent of the revenue is used to expand operations. The fish pond has a central role in the village food bank. Apart from fish, separate committees of the bank are responsible for the production of vegetables, chickens, ducks, and pigs.

The government expects to extend the pond program under the *Sixth National Economic and Social Development Plan*, to be in effect from 1987 to 1991, not only by strengthening the village ponds but also by promoting backyard and school ponds. School ponds will be used to supply inexpensive, nutritious food for school lunches, and also serve as instruments for teaching. It is expected that through collaboration with the Department of Teacher Education, ponds will be established at Teachers Training Colleges in order to familiarize new and in-service teachers with their technology and management. Loei Teachers College in the Northeast region of Thailand, for example, is preparing seven different-sized ponds with advice from the Provincial Fisheries Office. The office and the college will work together in the development of ponds in the primary schools in the provinces of Khan Kaen and Loei.

A World Bank study suggested that in nutrition Thailand's "actions in the past have mostly focused on interventions through the health delivery system" and thus "a broader approach is required, linking nutritional considerations with agricultural and food policies."[11] In its heavy emphasis on nutrition-oriented village fish ponds, the Government of Thailand has now in fact become a leader in showing explicit concern for the alleviation of malnutrition as a matter of policy in the fisheries sector.

NOTES

1. Amorn Nondasuta et al., *Nutrition in Primary Health Care* (Bangkok: Ministry of Public Health, 1984) p. 19.
2. Government of Thailand, *The Fifth National Economic and Social Development Plan (1982-1986)* (Bangkok: National Economic and Social Development Board, Office of the Prime Minister, 1981), pp. 392-401. The plan gave very little attention to fisheries development.
3. Government of Thailand, *The Fifth National Economic and Social Development Plan (1982-1986)*, p. 514.
4. Lars Herborg, *The Feasibility of Producing Roller Dried Fish in Thailand* (FAO Consultancy Report, 1983), pp. 15, 17.
5. James E. Austin and Christopher Mock, "High-Protein Product Development in Thailand," in James E. Austin, ed., *Nutrition Programs in the Third World: Cases and Readings*, (Cambridge, Massachusetts: Oelgeschlager, Gunn and Hain, 1981), pp. 151-175. Also see "Local Production in Thailand?" *International FPC News*, No. 13 (April 1984), pp. 4-5.
6. Herborg, *The Feasibility of Producing Roller Dried Fish in Thailand*, p. 16. At the time of this study, US$1 = 23 baht.
7. Jesse M. Floyd, *The Role of Fish in Nutrition in Four Selected Countries of Southeast Asia*. Consultant's report to the Food Policy and Nutrition Division (Rome: FAO, 1984), p. 68.
8. A similar pattern has occurred with rice. From 1970 to 1980 rice production increased 31 percent, but exports increased 263 percent. This in combination with the population increase led to a decline in per capita rice availability of 18.5 percent over the period. Thailand's food balance sheets do not indicate any compensation from other food items. See Rahmat U. Qureshi, *Nutrition Considerations in*

Agriculture (Bangkok: FAO Regional Office for Asia and the Pacific, 1982).

9. Elizabeth D. Samson, "Fisheries," in George Kent and Mark J. Valencia, eds., *Marine Policy in Southeast Asia* (Berkeley: University of California Press, 1984).

10. Bung-Orn Saisithi, "Thailand," in *Fish By-Catch . . . Bonus from the Sea* (Ottawa, Canada: International Development Research Centre/Food and Agriculture Organization of the United Nations, 1982), pp. 143-146.

11. World Bank, *Thailand: Managing Public Resources for Structural Adjustment* (Washington, D.C.: WB, 1984), p. 259.

Chapter 7

INDIA

In a 1966 survey of possibilities for increasing food production to meet India's minimum nutritional requirements, it was observed that fish "is the one item in our requirements of food that has the largest potential for increased production causing, at the same time, no strain on India's limited land resources. . . . For a country with such low levels, qualitatively of food consumption, as India, fish ought to command high priority in the solution of India's long term food problem."[1] To suggest how a national program might be formulated for making better use of India's vast potential in fisheries, this introduction is followed by a brief account of the current pattern of production and disposition of fisheries products in India. In the third section India's nutrition and malnutrition are described. The fourth section distinguishes the three major phases of fisheries operations--production, processing, and distribution--and describes actions that could be taken in each to help alleviate malnutrition in India. The fifth and concluding section discusses how such action could be undertaken within a comprehensive national program designed to increase the contribution of fisheries to the alleviation of malnutrition in India.

There is not enough fish available in India. Projections show that in the future the supply of fish may fall far short of meeting the demand.[2] The studies which make these projections urge that something should be done to increase production and thus minimize the anticipated shortfall. Their concern is primarily with market demand, demand that is backed up by purchasing power. Here, however, the purpose is to find ways to

84

respond to current problems of malnutrition. The concern is with the problem of meeting needs as distinguished from fulfilling market demand.

PRODUCTION AND DISPOSITION

In 1983 India produced about 2,520,000 metric tons of fisheries products, more than in any preceding year. India's catch constituted about 3.3 percent of that year's world total catch of 76,470,600 metric tons.[3]

India's marine fisheries include a traditional sector operating inshore with non-mechanized craft, a modern sector consisting of small motorized boats operating nearshore, and an ultramodern sector consisting of large motorized vessels capable of operating in deep seas far offshore. The traditional sector accounts for about two-thirds of the total volume of production and most of the employment in fisheries production.

India's inland fisheries consist of capture and culture fisheries operating in rivers, lakes, irrigation canals, tanks, and reservoirs. Except for river fishing, "the inland water resources of the country, by and large, are under-exploited. The yield levels are far below the potential yields."[4] State governments have been doing a great deal to promote culture fisheries through the establishment of Fish Farmers' Development Agencies, providing subsidies for renovation of tanks, and providing subsidized seed supplies.

Fish goes into the domestic food supply, into non-food uses such as fish meal for animal feed, and into export. In 1979-1981 about 88 percent of the total quantity of fish produced in India was used (either fresh or dry) for domestic food supply, about 8 percent went to non-food uses, and about 6 percent was exported. No significant quantity of fish was imported.[5]

Fish Consumption

In 1974-76 fish accounted for 22.4 percent of India's animal protein supply, a relatively large share.

However, since the level of animal protein consumption in India is low, fish accounted for only 2.3 percent of the total protein supply.[6] Fish accounts for only a small share of the diet. On a national basis the supply per person is only about three kilograms per year. India ranks 136th among 162 countries in fish supply per capita, a level even lower than that of many landlocked countries.[7]

This low level of supply may be surprising, but it is even more extraordinary when set against the fact that in recent years India has ranked as the seventh largest fish producing nation in the world, behind only Japan, the Soviet Union, China, the United States, Chile, and Norway.[8] India as a nation is a large producer of fish but, with its population of over 700 million, on a per capita basis it is only a small producer. Only about 3.4 kilograms per person are produced each year. Technically much more fish could be produced, particularly from the 200 nautical-mile Exclusive Economic Zone which India declared in 1977 and from underutilized inland water resources.

Of course fish consumption is much higher in some areas than in others. Fish constitutes an important part of the diet in many coastal areas of India, particularly in the fish-consuming southern states: Andhra Pradesh, Karnataka, Kerala, Orissa, Tamil Nadu, and West Bengal. The coastal states and union territories, with only half of the country's population, together account for almost 98 percent of the domestic consumption of marine fish.[9] As Table 7.1 shows, in the 1960s Kerala was the major fish consuming state:

In Kerala over 77 per cent reported fish consumption. Even in the lower income groups the proportion of families that consumed fish was as high as that observed among the lower/middle and the middle income groups and it was higher than that observed in the upper income group. Fish is the major source of animal protein.[10]

The high levels of fish consumption in Kerala have been partly due to the low price of fish. In a comparison

Table 7.1

Proportion of Families Consuming Fish Preparations (percentage) and Average Daily Quantity of Fish Consumed in Selected Southern States (grams)

| State | ....Income Group............ | | | |
	Low	Lower Middle	Middle	Upper
Kerala				
families (%)	76.5	78.4	79.6	72.3
consumption (g)	99.7	101.3	130.3	153.1
Andhra Pradesh				
families (%)	3.5	3.4	4.7	1.6
consumption (g)	5.1	5.3	6.3	2.1
Karnataka				
families (%)	13.1	7.9	9.2	6.1
consumption (g)	14.5	12.8	12.9	11.0
Tamil Nadu				
families (%)	5.1	6.2	5.8	8.7
consumption (g)	5.3	8.4	4.8	7.8

Source: Protein Foods Association of India, *Food Habits Survey*, 1969, as reported in C. H. Shah, S. D. Sawant, and B. I. Sanghavi, *Nutrition Gap: An Economic Analysis* (Bombay: Himalaya Publishing House, 1983), pp. 37–39, 47–50.

of many different foods, whitebait fish yielded far more protein per rupee than any other animal product. The only cheaper protein sources in terms of protein yield per rupee were Bengal gram (*dhal*), and cow peas, both of which are significantly inferior protein sources.[11]

Fish consumption in Kerala probably has declined since these data were collected as a result of the increasing relative price of fish:

> Kerala's population is essentially a fish-eating population; the level of fish consumption in Kerala is four times the national average. Until very recently fish was a relatively cheap source of protein. In the early part of the 1970s, fish consumption stood at 15 kg per capita per annum. This figure has, however, been declining, but the fact remains that even in the humblest of households there is at least one meal with fish.[12]

Exports

India's fish exports have grown rapidly, partly because of the active promotional efforts of the Marine Products Export Development Authority (MPEDA) established in 1972. From 1961 to 1979 the quantity of exports increased at 10.2 percent per year, and from 1974 to 1979 at 14.5 percent per year.[13] The growth in the value of exports has increased even more rapidly.[14] In 1981 the average price of exported marine fish was five times the average domestic price. The largest foreign exchange earners have been shrimp, froglegs, and lobster.

Shrimp has been dominant, accounting for 87 percent of the export value and 72 percent of the export quantity in 1981.[15] In 1983 it was reported that "India has remained the world's largest producer of shrimps during the last decade, except in 1972 . . . and in 1978 and 1981 . . . . It is also the world's largest exporter of shrimp in quantity terms."[16] India has been the largest supplier of shrimp to Japan and one of the largest suppliers of shrimp to the United States, following only Mexico,

Ecuador, and Panama. In 1985 India provided the United States with over 42 million dollars worth of shrimp.[17]

In the early 1980s there was some stagnation of export growth, due largely to competition from other developing countries in the world shrimp market. The decline has also been partly due to declining yields from overexploited nearshore shrimp fisheries.

The export of fisheries products is warranted for products such as shrimp which draw high prices overseas and for which there is little domestic demand. (Before the shrimp export trade began in the early 1960s, shrimp was used as fertilizer for coconut trees.) However, the promotion of exports can sometimes go too far and have significant negative effects on domestic nutrition.

In India and elsewhere, many export fisheries are quite independent of fisheries for domestic markets. For example, offshore fisheries for export products may have no noticeable impact on inshore traditional fisheries or on domestic consumers. In some cases, however, the linkages may be very significant. Large trawlers seeking products for export often operate near shore, thus interfering with small-scale fishing operations. Apart from direct conflict on the fishing grounds, there may be competition for labor, for capital, for processing and marketing infrastructure, and for governmental support. As more of the productive resources available to the fishing industry are devoted to producing for middle and upper classes, whether within the country or abroad, less is produced for the bottom end of the market.[18]

Prices

Tables 7.2 and 7.3 provide data on disposition and relative prices for marine fish alone. As Singh and Gupta observe with regard to these data:

> It is important to note that there was a continuous decline in the share of production of domestic fresh fish in the total marine fish production. The share of domestic fresh fish consumption was 71.2 per cent in 1966. It declined to 43 per cent in 1978-79.

TABLE 7.2

Utilization Pattern of Marine Fish in India

Year	Fresh	Dry Edible	Fish Meal	Export	Total
	(%)	(%)	(%)	(%)	(m.t.)
1966	71.2	17.8	7.2	3.8	890,300
1969	57.5	25.0	11.4	6.1	913,600
1972	50.1	29.2	13.8	6.9	980,000
1975	47.5	31.0	14.1	7.4	1,422,700
1978-79	43.0	31.5	14.7	10.8	1,529,700

Source: Amarjeet Singh and V. K. Gupta, "Marketing of Marine Fish: Some Policy Issues," in U. K. Srivastava and M. Dharma Reddy, eds., *Fisheries Development in India: Some Aspects of Policy Management* (New Delhi: Concept Publishing Company, 1983), p. 106.

TABLE 7.3

Annual Average Indices of Wholesale Prices of Fish, Food, and All Commodities (1961–62 = 100)

Year	..........Price Indices of............		
	Fish	Food Articles	All Commodities
1970-71	---	203.9	181.1
1971-72	384.9	210.3	188.4
1972-73	484.7	239.5	207.1
1973-74	757.1	295.6	254.3
1974-75	1021.3	364.0	313.9
1975-76	1271.3	347.7	302.7
1976-77	1397.4	330.1	310.7
1977-78	1599.0	368.9	336.5
1978-79	1851.4	366.4	366.5

Source: Amarjeet Singh and V. K. Gupta, "Marketing of Marine Fish: Some Policy Issues," in U. K. Srivastava and M. Dharma Reddy, eds., Fisheries Development in India: Some Aspects of Policy Management (New Delhi: Concept Publishing Company, 1983), p. 105.

As a result, the availability of the net domestic fresh fish virtually remained almost static between 1966 and 1978-79. This resulted in a steep rise in the fish price indices. Price indices of fish reached 1851.4 (base 1961-1962) during 1978-79 as against 366.4 for food articles and 366.5 for all commodities.[19]

Exports can be judged excessive when they result in noticeable increases in domestic fish prices. As shown above in Table 7.3, fish prices have indeed increased in India. Many expert observers attribute this increase to the rapid increase in fish exports:

> The developmental efforts in the fishing industry, notwithstanding the objective of increased domestic supplies of protein rich foods at reasonable prices, have led mainly to an increase in exports over the years. Despite the growth of fish landings at an annual rate of 3.5 per cent the domestic markets have faced shortages of fish and fish products, and consequent fast rising prices. It is now being realized that increased landings do not necessarily result in increased supplies in domestic markets, particularly for human consumption.[20]

The studies which make projections into the future and predict shortfalls in supplies ask what would happen if prices remained relatively constant. In reality, there never is an actual gap. When supplies are short, prices go up, and effective demand is reduced to match whatever supply may be available. In India, partly because of exports, supplies have become short and prices have gone up.

It should not be assumed that with decreasing supplies and increasing prices everyone reduces consumption by a similar amount. The supply which remains moves toward the wealthier classes, so that the poor suffer the greatest reductions in supply.

It might be argued that India has turned to exports because its domestic market is saturated. Market demand may have been met, but this does not mean that needs have been fulfilled. The apparent saturation of the market is an artifact of low purchasing power. If Indians had the means they undoubtedly would purchase and consume far more fish than they do now.

NUTRITION

Cereals and Pulses

The Indian diet is based on cereals. Rice and wheat are the most important staple foods, but a variety of coarse grains such as barley, corn, millet, and sorghum are important in many areas. Rice and wheat production have increased rapidly since the 1970s, largely due to the adoption of high-yielding varieties of rice and wheat in India's "green revolution." As a result, domestic food-grain stocks have been kept at high levels, and since 1979 India has been a substantial exporter of rice and wheat.

Pulses such as lentils are important for the poor, especially for the protein they provide. Thus it is significant that "there has been a long-run secular decline in pulse production as the area cultivated in more profitable crops, including rice and wheat, has expanded. Because of the role of pulses in providing low-cost protein, this decline is a continuing problem for the Indian agricultural sector."[21] Similarly, the increasing production of wheat and rice at the expense of coarse grains undoubtedly results in an overall shift of grain supplies away from the poor.

Animal Foods

Historically, animal protein sources such as fish, meat, eggs, and milk have played a very small role in the diet of the average Indian. However, the majority of Indians are not wholly averse to eating meat:

In fact, nutritional surveys have shown that 71 per cent of the people could be called non-vegetarians if consuming meat even once in a year could be so defined, and undoubtedly lack of purchasing power is a major factor in the dominance of the vegetarian diet in India. But it is also a fact that economics alone is not the reason for choosing a vegetarian diet. There is a real preference for a vegetarian diet in India, not only among Hindus but also among other communities like Christians and Muslims . . . Vegetarianism is a part of the Indian tradition.[22]

Perhaps the surest way to estimate the extent to which the operative constraints are economic rather than religious and cultural would be to determine the price and income elasticities of demand for animal products for different economic classes and for different religious and cultural groups.[23]

Malnutrition

India can now claim to be self-sufficient in rice and wheat in the sense that bulk imports of these cereals are no longer undertaken on a regular basis. With the large buffer stocks that are now maintained, the threat of famine from episodic disturbances in supplies has been greatly diminished. However, these achievements do not mean that the problem of chronic malnutrition has been solved. On the basis of a variety of definitions and measurement techniques, estimates of the proportion of the population affected by malnutrition range from about 15 percent to about 50 percent.[24] India's *Sixth Five Year Plan, 1980-1985* acknowledges that:

The problem of malnutrition is widely prevalent across the various socio-economic groups, particularly among those below the poverty line, landless agricultural labourers, people in slum and remote tribal areas and those who are affected by constant calamities like drought . . . . Children, pregnant women and nursing mothers are seriously affected by malnutrition . . . .[25]

The *Seventh Five Year Plan* reports:

> Dietary surveys by the National Nutrition Monitoring Bureau reveal that nearly 50 per cent of the households surveyed in different States of the country consume food which is quite inadequate to meet their requirements of either calories or proteins, or even both. An assessment of malnutrition among children below 6 years of age reveals that less than 15 per cent of them could be considered as having a normal status of nutrition; the rest suffer from varying degrees of under-nutrition.[26]

Most apparent protein deficiency encountered in India and elsewhere is associated with deficiency in energy intake. In a study done in Kerala, however, a little over 10 percent of the people sampled had pure protein deficiency: their intake of energy food was adequate but their protein intake was inadequate. Most of the cases were among children and among expectant and lactating mothers.[27] Protein intake levels on the average and for the low income group in Kerala were the lowest in the four states surveyed. The existence of protein deficiencies in Kerala despite the very high average level of fish consumption might be explained by a significant skew in the distribution of the fish consumed.

Remedies

To augment the general development efforts that have been undertaken, many different programs have been launched specifically to combat malnutrition. For example, the distribution of grains is partly controlled by the government's Food Corporation of India (FCI). The FCI purchases grain domestically or imports it and then markets it at controlled prices through a network of over 200,000 fair-price shops. In some years the public distribution has accounted for almost a fifth of all food grains available.[28] Many states also have organized public food distribution programs.

In the first three national five year plans spanning the period 1951 to 1966, nutrition formed one of the components of the health sector. However:

> In the Fourth Plan an Integrated Nutrition Programme . . . was introduced. It was observed that production of "more food" was needed. Stress was laid on the development of agriculture along with animal husbandry and fisheries . . . . The Applied Nutrition Programme (ANP) was first introduced in 1960 . . . . This programme was introduced to spread the concept of balanced diet, production and consumption of protective foods and proper techniques of cooking. The Special Nutrition Program (SNP) was introduced in 1970-71 as a crash scheme . . . . The mid-day meals programme which was initiated in 1962-63 was extended in subsequent years. It provides supplementary nutrition of 300 calories with 8-12 grams of protein to children in the age group of 6-11 years.[29]

The Special Nutrition Program and the Mid-Day Meals Program are the major nutrition activities in the overall Minimum Needs Program (MNP). Food is also distributed through the Food for Work Program, now the National Rural Employment Program. The program uses grain as wages to pay for labor devoted to building public works such as roads and dams.

By 1980 the Special Nutrition Programme had reached over 8.2 million children, pregnant women, and nursing mothers. The Mid-Day Meals program had reached over 13 million children. However, there has been general disappointment with the effectiveness of these and other nutrition programs that have been undertaken.

In 1975 Integrated Child Development Services (ICDS) was launched to provide health and educational services to small children and pregnant and lactating women. Services are delivered at village focal points called *anganwadis*--courtyards for child care. Nutrition-related interventions include nutritional supplements, immunizations, health checkups, and primary medical care.

The program appears to be effective in reducing the incidence of malnutrition.

It seems clear that ending malnutrition will require ending poverty. It seems equally clear that, in the interim, direct nutrition intervention programs will still be necessary.

POLICY OPTIONS

India's fisheries policies now are oriented much more to producers than to consumers. Indeed, the objectives of fisheries development as listed in the Seventh Plan speak primarily of increasing production and give some attention to improving the socio-economic conditions of fishermen, but give practically no attention to the fulfillment of nutritional needs. "The main thrust will be on exploitation of the EEZ," the 200 nautical-mile exclusive economic zone.[30]

The plan says that:

> To produce more nutritive food in the country and to generate employment in rural areas for the weaker sections of society, accelerated growth in the fisheries sector is envisaged during the Seventh Plan period.

It is not clear how the benefits of this growth are to be directed toward the weaker sections. That increased production of food does not in itself assure that it will be consumed by those who need it most should be clear from India's recent history in agriculture, in which "the low purchasing power of large numbers of consumers has meant that many people have not been able to increase their food intake and that inadequate nutrition continues to coexist with production 'surpluses'."[31]

Fisheries could make a larger contribution to the alleviation of malnutrition in India in the three major interacting phases of production (catching or culturing), processing, and distribution. These activities could at the same time help develop the fishing industry itself.

Production

The potential contributions of India's fisheries are very different in the modern and traditional sectors of marine fisheries and in the various kinds of inland fisheries.

In the marine fisheries, the modern sectors yield higher foreign exchange earnings, but the traditional sectors make a much larger contribution to domestic food supplies, especially for the rural poor. Since the 1970s the government has provided strong support for the development of the modern export-oriented fishing industry, but it has not provided comparable support for fisheries producing for domestic consumption. (Support might be in the form of technical assistance, infrastructure development, extension services, or subsidies.) The support that has been provided has been directed at prospects with high commercial potentials. Some programs have been designed to protect small-scale fishing communities when they have been threatened by large-scale trawling operations encroaching on their customary nearshore fishing grounds. No help has been provided to traditional fisheries specifically because of their contribution to fulfilling local nutritional needs. Re-examination of that contribution might indicate that increased support of some traditional fisheries would be warranted not for conventional economic reasons but because they can--and already do--help in alleviating local malnutrition.

The modern sectors supply great quantities of low cost, popular species such as seer, Indian mackerel, and sardine. Conceivably they could pursue presently underutilized species, especially in the still-underexploited Exclusive Economic Zone. However, because they are capital-intensive and because they are linked to major marketing networks, the large-scale private operations are consistently motivated to pursue the more highly profitable high cost species. In the absence of special subsidies for the purpose, the modern sector is not likely to take new initiatives in developing fisheries specializing in low cost products.

It now appears that the most promising new frontier for promoting nutrition-oriented fisheries production is in the inland fisheries, both capture and culture. These fisheries occupy otherwise underutilized surface area, and they can be undertaken near to the poor, rural population.

India has had considerable experience with introductions and stocking of lakes and reservoirs, with common carps (*Cyprinus carpio*), Chinese carps, gourami, tilapia (*Oreochromis hornorum*) and a variety of other species.[32] Many such efforts have been successful. However, success has been assessed in terms of levels of production and economic returns, not in terms of nutritional impacts. It would be useful if such programs were also explicitly and systematically assessed according to the extent to which they help alleviate local malnutrition.

Many people supplement their families' diets by subsistence fishing either along the coast or inland in publicly accessible waters. Government should take responsibility for intensive stocking of public waters with fish fry, not for commercial reasons, but for the significant nutritional benefits such stocking can yield for the poor. Where such operations are not actively managed the yield may be modest, but if the cost of stocking is very low that would not matter very much. In fact for the purpose of alleviating malnutrition the stocking of low value fish such as tilapia might be preferable to stocking high value fish; there might then be a higher likelihood that they would be left for the poor to catch. Repeated attempts to displace tilapia by introducing more "economic" species, particularly in Tamil Nadu, may have been a distinct disservice to the local poor.

Government should take positive steps to assure that the poor have free access to fish in public waters on a subsistence basis. Waters to which the poor traditionally have had free access should not be privatized to allow the culturing of products for export unless some alternative arrangements are made for the poor. There have been cases in Tamil Nadu, for example, in which waters were closed off to raise shrimp, thus shutting out the poor who previously had fished in there.

To assure some return on the effort invested, actively managed aquaculture operations cannot be undertaken in publicly accessible waters, but normally must be conducted in private or community controlled waters. Public waters sometimes can be used for private culturing operations through the use of pens or cages for the cultured fish, but these practices are not yet common in India.

In supporting inland fisheries through the Fish Farmers Development Agencies and other means, government should give special attention to those types of inland fisheries operations which make the most substantial contribution to alleviating malnutrition. These operations should be promoted and, where feasible they should be reproduced. Existing operations should be adapted to conform with the more effective kinds of operations.

Support for tank development sometimes takes the form of food-for-work programs administered by the Panchayat Unions. In the multipurpose rural development program undertaken by the World Food Programme in Mahendergarh District in Haryana, food-for-work was provided for the enlargement of existing ponds, excavation of water supply channels to link the irrigation canal system to those ponds, establishment of five regional nurseries, and the establishment of a model fish farm. Fish produced in these ponds were expected to be sold in the Delhi market.[33] Such food-for-work programs should also be used to create pond operations to produce fish for local consumption in poor rural areas. It would be especially fitting if the food-for-work rations included fish from successful neighboring ponds.

Policies regarding the right to fish in existing inland fisheries such as reservoirs vary a great deal from state to state, but the basic alternatives can be categorized as follows:

1. direct fishing by a government fishing authority;
2. lease by outright auction;
3. single lease on a royalty basis;
4. multiple licenses to fishers and fishers' cooperative societies.[34]

These methods for controlling access have different direct and indirect nutritional impacts on the local poor.

Leasing to individuals, for example, can result in an excessive concentration of benefits in the hands of the lessee, and thus raise strong local resentments:

> On one occasion, after the fish farmer had harvested the tank, the locals gathered around and refused to allow him to take the fish to be sold outside the village. They insisted that since the tank was common property they had the right to get the fish reared in it at half the market price offered in the town areas.[35]

The effects of different forms of control should be studied in very concrete terms and should be taken into account in the shaping of access policy. Considerations such as incomes to fishers and contractors, ease of management, environmental protection, and vulnerability to corruption should be taken into account, but at the same time nutritional effects should not ignored. The Central Inland Fisheries Research Institute, in its studies of the management aspects of inland fisheries, might be the appropriate lead agency for investigating the nutritional impacts of alternative forms of organization.

Aquaculture operations usually are conducted under private or governmental control, but they also can be operated by communities or cooperatives of some form. State governments in India could develop village and school fish pond programs similar to those in Thailand.

Not all inland fisheries make good contributions to the alleviation of malnutrition. Some allow for self-provisioning not by the poor but by the well-to-do, as in the case of farmers who use their irrigation wells to raise fish for themselves. Some are sound commercial ventures but have little effect on malnutrition because most of the product goes to consumers who are already well nourished. The prawn culturing operations, for example, have no direct nutritional benefit because the products are exported.

In promoting marine or inland fisheries for the purpose of alleviating malnutrition, it should be recognized that increasing production in a given area does not necessarily mean increasing supplies available for consumption in that area. While small-scale fishing operations are likely to sell in the immediate vicinity, highly commercialized operations are more likely to market their catch in major urban markets or export it. Even small-scale operations may have their products bought up by middlemen who transport them to larger towns and cities. To alleviate malnutrition, it is generally better to have local production for local consumption in order to limit costs of processing and distribution. Where feasible, production should be supported directly in those regions in which malnutrition is most prevalent.

Processing

Most fish consumed in India is fresh or preserved by sun-drying. Fish is also smoked, salted, and fermented. Freezing and canning are not carried out on a large scale except for the export market.

Canning and freezing generally are too expensive for products destined for poor people. Even if they were not expensive, they might not be advantageous for the poor. One major effect of preservation is that it increases the likelihood that the product will be shipped to markets at great distances from the point of production. Prices are so high in Calcutta, for example, that it draws fish from all over southern India, both east and west coasts. The modernization of fisheries in general, and improved preservation in particular, regularly result in moving fish away from the poor. Poor people in remote areas might not get any fish at all if it weren't so perishable.

However, there are some cases in which better processing might be helpful to the poor. Improvements in traditional low cost processing techniques can be sought specifically for those products that are favored by the poor but are not particularly attractive to the middle and upper classes. For example, work done at the College of Fisheries in Mangalore indicates that salted and pressed sardine and dried whitebait might provide higher quality dried fish than is obtained currently by sun-drying fish on the beach. This dried sardine product can be important for bridging the three-month monsoon period when fresh fish is not available. Undoubtedly there are many ways in which traditional preservation techniques can be improved to reduce wastage and improve the quality and durability of the product.

In India and elsewhere, much attention has been given to the improved utilization of "trash" fish so that instead of being discarded or used as animal feed it is used for human consumption. Processes have been developed for producing attractive edible products. For example, the Gujarat Fisheries Aquatic Sciences Research Institute has developed good quality salted and dried fish fillets with a long shelf life. The institute has also used trash fish to make fish protein concentrate, and used this product to make several different food items popular in Gujarat (*papad, papadi, chakri, sev, ganthia, sakkarpara,* salted biscuits).[36] Much of this sort of work in India and elsewhere has been geared to the preparation of products for the regular commercial market, and not for products targeted for the alleviation of malnutrition. However, some products such as the Gujarati fish fillets have been well received by the local poor. Whether products designed for the poor can be commercially viable remains an open question. If there is no subsidy, processing for middle class markets or for animal feed is likely to be more profitable.

Many inland fisheries suffer from very uneven production schedules. In some districts the tanks dry up in the summer, with the result that all have to be harvested almost simultaneously. Local demand is saturated and the fish farmers are obligated to dispose of the fish at very low prices, often to outsiders. If production schedules cannot be smoothed out, an alternative remedy would be to develop appropriate preservation techniques so that the fish can be consumed locally throughout the year.

Distribution

Fisheries products intended to be used to help alleviate malnutrition can be distributed through conventional marketing, through social (subsidized) marketing such as fair-price shops, through institutional feeding programs, or through established nutrition intervention programs. There is also the possibility of self-provisioning through subsistence fishing or backyard pond operations, but in such cases there is no distinct distribution phase.

If the open market is to be used to promote the use of fish to alleviate malnutrition, the key is to focus on low-cost products which are favored by the poor. Some forms of dried fish, for example, would be particularly suitable. New products such as the Gujarati fish fillets might be developed and promoted specifically for this purpose. With sound promotional programs, some of these fisheries products might prove to be commercially viable, and not require any direct subsidies at all.

A social marketing scheme specifically devoted to supplying poor customers with fish was established in Egypt in 1964. In India, social marketing of fisheries products could be conducted through the established system of fair-price shops. The products selected should have a high price elasticity of demand among the poor and a low price elasticity of demand among middle and upper class consumers. Otherwise anything that is done to reduce prices would subsidize middle and upper classes as well.

Marketing services should be attentive not only to prices but also to delivery mechanisms to assure that poor communities have ready access to points of sale. Support services should be provided to fish retailers and vendors in poor areas.

Institutional feeding programs include all programs in which the delivery of food to consumers is organized by persons other than the consumers themselves. Such feeding programs may be found in schools, prisons, hospitals, and many other contexts. In institutional feeding programs, decisions regarding the choice of foods are made by a manager rather than by the final consumers. The manager is likely to be acutely cost conscious, and he or she is likely to be more concerned with the nutritional value of the food that is purchased than the average consumer.

While they do not reach the large numbers of poor children who do not attend school, school lunch programs can be useful for reaching some mildly or moderately malnourished children. The Mid-Day Meals Program already underway in India provides a good opportunity for delivering appropriate fisheries products. Day care centers for pre-school children, congregate dining arrangements for adults, take-home meals, or home-delivered meals and other direct feeding programs should be considered as well.

Commercial fisheries production and processing operations generally are most responsive to the middle and upper classes because they have the money to create a market demand. However, the production of uniform products in very large numbers for institutional feeding programs can make it profitable to be responsive to the needs of the poor. Such programs are commercially attractive because of the consolidation of demand in a single decision-making center, resulting in potentially large economies of scale. The fact that school lunch programs often are subsidized adds to their commercial attractiveness.

Established nutrition intervention programs, whether within or outside the Mid-Day Meals Program and the Special Nutrition Program should be reviewed to determine whether some form of fish product might be suitable for the protein component. For example, the preserved sardine and whitebait being developed at the College of Fisheries in Mangalore might be used in the local anganwadi program for providing food to needy women and children. Also, fish might be used as part of the ration in food-for-work programs such as those sponsored by the World Food Programme.

ACTION PROGRAM

Food policy experts agree that the problem of malnutrition in India cannot be solved simply by increasing overall food production. It is important to also assure that the incomes of the poor increase so that they can obtain the food that is produced.[37] Fisheries development can make a great contribution in this respect by providing adequate levels of income to workers in the industry. In that approach, however, fish is simply another commodity.

The fact that the product is food is irrelevant to the producer because it is sold rather than eaten. The emphasis in this study, in contrast, is on ways in which fish as food could make a greater contribution to the alleviation of malnutrition.

The states of India vary in their physical endowments, cultures, level and nature of malnutrition, and interest in fisheries products. In some areas the price elasticities of demand for fish are high and in others they are low. With these great variations among the states of India, there cannot be any generally applicable program regarding the use of fisheries in alleviating malnutrition. The major work will properly be at the state level. However, the national government could do a great deal to provide leadership and support for the effort.

Historically, national planning for food and nutrition in India has focused on cereals, pulses, edible oils, and milk. In view of the low level of consumption of protein from animal sources and the high potential of fisheries resources, it might be timely for the government of India to formulate a systematic program for the use of fisheries products for the alleviation of malnutrition.

A national level program could begin with governmental endorsement of increasing use of fisheries for alleviating malnutrition. This could be included as one of the explicit objectives of fisheries development. The national government could help to identify the major types of activities through which fisheries could make a larger contribution to the alleviation of malnutrition. Model programs could be designed and implemented at the state level with the assistance of the national government.

Action in the production, processing, and distribution stages of fishing operations would have to be shaped to fit specific local circumstances. It should not be expected that new nutrition intervention programs would be devised specifically for the purpose of using fisheries products. Rather, existing activities in fisheries and in nutrition should be reviewed to assess how they might be adapted to make more effective use of fisheries products for the alleviation of malnutrition. For example, modest changes in the management of established reservoir fisheries might strengthen their local nutritional impacts. The fair-price shops might be used as a major distribution outlet for selected products. Direct feeding programs such as the Special Nutrition Program and the Mid-Day Meals Program could be examined to see whether some form of fisheries product might be used for the protein component. Prevailing practices in the feeding of fisheries products to small children could be studied to determine how they might be improved. Of course the local poor should be fully engaged in the planning of new or adapted programs.

If fish is to make a larger contribution to the alleviation of malnutrition in India, systematic and deliberate efforts would have to be undertaken to connect those most vulnerable to malnutrition with suitable supplies of fisheries products. In order to strengthen the linkages it would be necessary to identify target groups with concretely assessed nutritional deficiencies, to identify particular fisheries products which could meet those needs, and to carefully design programs to provide those products to those who need them, whether through market or non-market mechanisms. Some of the policy options have been outlined here. A decisive action program could be formulated, perhaps in the context of preparation for India's eighth five-year development plan. With appropriate leadership from the national government, particularly from the Department of Fisheries, and with good coordination among interested agencies both within and outside of government, a coherent and effective program could be mounted.

NOTES

1. V. K. R. V. Rao, *Food, Nutrition, and Poverty in India* (New Delhi: Vikas Publishing House, 1982), p. 49.

2. S. Sreenivasa Rao, "An Overview of the Marine Fish Marketing in India," and "M. Raghavachari, "Marine Fish Supplies: Trends and Projections," in U. K. Srivastava and M. Dharma Reddy, eds., *Fisheries Development in India: Some Aspects of Policy Management* (New Delhi: Concept Publishing Company, 1983), pp. 3-23 and pp. 61-99.
3. Food and Agriculture Organization of the United Nations, *1983 Yearbook of Fisheries Statistics: Catches and Landings* (Rome: FAO, 1984), p. 72.
4. M. L. Dantwala, "Foreword," in Srivastava and Reddy, *Fisheries Development in India*, p. vi.
5. Food and Agriculture Organization of the United Nations, *1983 Yearbook of Fishery Statistics: Fishery Commodities* (Rome: FAO, 1984), p. 175.
6. Helga Josupeit, *The Economic and Social Effects of the Fishing Industry: A Comparative Study* (Rome: FAO Fisheries Circular No. 314, Revision 1, 1981), pp. 5-7.
7. Food and Agriculture Organization of the United Nations, *1983 Yearbook of Fishery Statistics: Fishery Commodities*, Vol. 57 (Rome: FAO, 1985), pp. 73-75.
8. Food and Agriculture Organization of the United Nation, *1984 Yearbook of Fishery Statistics: Fishery Commodities*, Vol. 59 (Rome: FAO, 1986), pp. 253-256.
9. V. K. Gupta, et al., *Marine Fish Marketing in India: Volume I. Summary and Conclusions* (Ahmedabad: Indian Institute of Management, 1984), p. 49. This comprehensive six-volume study of marketing aspects of India's marine fisheries has been followed with an *All-India Inland Fish Marketing Study*, also undertaken by the Indian Institute of Management.
10. C. H. Shah, S. D. Sawant, and B. I. Sanghavi, *Nutrition Gap: An Economic Analysis* (Bombay: Himalaya Publishing House, 1983), pp. 27-28.
11. Shah, Sawant, and Sanghavi, *Nutrition Gap*, pp. 99-100.
12. Leela Gulati, *Women in Fishing Villages on the Kerala Coast: Demographic and Socio-Economic Impacts of*

a Fisheries Development Project (Geneva: World Employment Programme Working Paper No. 128, International Labour Organisation, 1983), p. 4.

13. G. S. Gupta, P. S. George, and B. Subrahmanyam, "Marine Fish: Consumer Behavior and Demand Forecasts," in Srivastava and Reddy, *Fisheries Development in India*, p. 53.

14. Gupta et al., in *Marine Fish Marketing in India, Vol. III*, say (on p. 80) that marine fish "export increased by more than five fold in quantity and by more than six fold in value between 1961 and 1979." However, this estimate of the increase in value does not take account of inflation in the value of the rupee over the time period.

15. S. N. Rao, "Product Development for Export," in Srivastava and Reddy, *Fisheries Development in India*, pp. 211-218.

16. *Shrimps: A Survey of the World Market* (Geneva: International Trade Centre UNCTAD/GATT, 1983), p. 46.

17. National Marine Fisheries Service, *Fisheries of the United States 1985* (Washington, D.C.: NMFS, 1986), p. 55.

18. These linkages are analyzed for Southeast Asia in Jesse M. Floyd, *The Political Economy of Fisheries Development in Indonesia, Malaysia, the Philippines, and Thailand* (Honolulu: Doctoral dissertation in Political Science, 1985).

19. Amarjeet Singh and V. K. Gupta, "Marketing of Marine Fish: Some Policy Issues," in Srivastava and Reddy, *Fisheries Development in India*, p. 104.

20. U. K. Srivastava and M. Dharma, "Editor's Note," in Srivastava and Reddy, *Fisheries Development in India*, p. vi.

21. John A. Dixon and Rodney Tyers, "India's Food Security: Supply, Demand, and Signs of Success" in Anthony H. Chisholm and Rodney Tyers, eds., *Food Security: Theory, Policy, and Perspectives from Asia and the Pacific Rim* (Lexington, Massachusetts: Lexington Books, 1982), p. 194.

22. Rao, *Food, Nutrition, and Poverty in India*, p. 146.

23. Religious and cultural constraints on fish consumption are described in F. J. Simoons, "Fish as Forbidden Food: The Case of India," *Ecology of Food and Nutrition*, Vol. 3 (1974), pp. 185-201.

24. Some of the measurement and analysis problems are described in P. V. Sukhatme, ed., *New Concepts in Nutrition and Their Implications for Policy* (Pune: Maharashtra Association for the Cultivation of Science, 1982). Also see Shah, Sawant, and Sanghavi, *Nutrition Gap*.

25. Government of India, Planning Commission, *Sixth Five Year Plan, 1980-85* (New Delhi: Government of India, 1981), p. 377.

26. Government of India, Planning Commission, *Seventh Five Year Plan, 1985-90, Vol. II* (New Delhi: Government of India, 1985), p. 313.

27. Shah, Sawant, and Sanghavi, *Nutrition Gap*, pp. 126, 132-133. Food consumption surveys consistently show Kerala to rank lowest among Indian states in energy and protein intake. However, it ranks high in most health indicators. See C. R. Soman, "Inter-relationship between Fertility, Mortality and Nutrition--The Kerala Experience," in Sukhatme, ed., *New Concepts in Nutrition and Their Implications for Policy*, pp. 223-234.

28. A detailed account by a former chairman of FCI is provided in R. N. Chopra, *Evolution of Food Policy in India* (New Delhi: Macmillan India Limited, 1981).

29. *Sixth Plan*, p. 378. Also see p. 225.

30. Government of India, Planning Commission, *Seventh Five Year Plan, 1985-90, Vol. II* (New Delhi: Government of India, 1985), pp. 34-36.

31. Dixon and Tyers, "India's Food Security . . . ," p. 192.

32. Indo-Pacific Fishery Commission (IPFC), *Report of the Joint Workshop of the IPFC Working Party on Inland Fisheries and the IPFC Working Party on Aquaculture on the Role of Stocking and Introductions in the Improvement of Production of Lakes and Reservoirs, New Delhi, India, 24-25 January 1984*

110

(Rome: Food and Agriculture Organization of the United Nations, 1984).

33. *World Food Programme Assistance for Fisheries Development in Third World Countries and The Use of Fish Products in Food Aid* (Rome: World Food Programme, 1984), p. 25.

34. Pradeep K. Yadav, "Reservoir Fishery Management: Major Policy Issues for Government Intervention," in Srivastava and Reddy, *Fisheries Development in India*, pp. 433-457.

35. John Kurien, *Pisiculture Potentials in Dharmapuri District, Tamilnadu* (Trivandrum: Centre for Development Studies, 1980), pp. 12-13.

36. Niranjan D. Chhaya, "Recent Advances in Commercial Utilization of Trash Fish for Edible Use in Gujarat," in Srivastava and Reddy, *Fisheries Development in India*, pp. 203-210. Also see Gupta, *Marine Fish Marketing in India, Volume I*, pp. 84-85.

37. John W. Mellor, *The New Economics of Growth--A Strategy for India and the Developing World* (Ithaca, New York: Cornell University Press, 1976). Also see V. K. R. V. Rao and John Dixon, cited earlier.

Chapter 8

SOUTHERN AFRICA

Fisheries resources could make a substantially greater contribution to the alleviation of malnutrition in Africa. This chapter reviews the potentials for the nine countries of the Southern African Development Coordination Conference (SADCC): Angola, Botswana, Lesotho, Malawi, Mozambique, Swaziland, Tanzania, Zambia, and Zimbabwe. These "frontline" countries, facing South Africa, have not suffered the extreme famine experienced in eastern Africa, but their problems are similar to those of eastern Africa in that several of them must deal with continuing internal political turmoil which severely inhibits their development. The nations of southern Africa have also had to deal with great pressures from South Africa.

SADCC

SADCC was established by the nine member countries at a meeting in Lusaka in April 1980, when Zimbabwe attained independence. The objectives set out in the Lusaka Declaration, "Southern Africa: Toward Economic Liberation," were:

1. the reduction of economic dependence, particularly but not only, on the Republic of South Africa;

2. the forging of links to create a genuine and equitable regional integration;

111

3. the mobilization of resources to promote
   the implementation of national, interstate
   and regional policies;

4. concerted action to secure international
   cooperation within the framework of
   their strategy for economic liberation.

SADCC is organized on a decentralized basis, with responsibility for different sectors divided among the member countries. The sectoral coordinator for fisheries is the Government of Malawi.

SADCC has already formulated a number of fisheries project proposals, most of which are awaiting funding. Their broad scope is conveyed by the list of project titles, as listed in SADCC's Food and Agriculture report of January 1986:

1. Regional Fish Production, Processing and
   Marketing Survey.

2. Study to Identify Regional Projects/
   Programmes of Production and/or Com-
   mercialisation of Fishing and Fish Processing Materials and Equipment.

3. Fisheries Administrative Support Unit.

4. Fisheries Program Planning Support.

5. Regional Fisheries Training Project.

6. Regional Fisheries Documentation Centre.

7. Fisheries Investigation in Botswana.

8. Integrated Fish-cum-Duck Farming in
   Lesotho.

9. Joint Research of Pelagic Fishery
   Resources of Lake Niassa/Malawi--
   Malawi/Mozambique/Tanzania.

10. Integrated Pig-Fish Farming Development and Research Project.

11. Lake Kariba Fisheries Research and Development--Zambia/Zimbabwe.

COUNTRY PROFILES

Summary data on the SADCC countries are provided in Table 8.1. Further information may be found in the FAO *Fishery Country Profiles.*[1]

Angola

Before its independence in November 1975 about 85 percent of Angola's marine catch was reduced to fish meal and oil, but the new government has decided to give high priority to the utilization of fish for direct human consumption. About 80 percent of the total catch off Angola is taken by vessels of other countries, primarily the USSR, Spain, and Italy. In accordance with their contractual obligations, most of these countries land between 30 and 50 percent of their catches locally. Angola imports substantial quantities of canned sardines, tuna, and mackerel from Portugal, Spain, and Japan.

Inland fishing in Angola's extensive river system is largely a subsistence activity. It yields about 6,000 tons a year, but the potential is estimated at about 50,000 tons.

Fish, which in the mid-1970s accounted for about one-fourth of the total animal protein intake, is important in the Angolan diet. Its contribution could be increased substantially with fuller use of inland fisheries resources and improved distribution and marketing infrastructure.

Angola has great potential for increasing its fisheries production, but it will be difficult to exploit until after political stability is established.

TABLE 8.1

SADCC Country Data

	Ango-la	Bot-swana	Leso-tho	Mala-wi	Mozam-bique	Swazi-land	Tan-zania	Zam-bia	Zimba-bwe
Area ('000 km²)	1247	600	30	118	784	17	945	753	390
Shelf area to 200 nautical miles ('000 km²)	..51	0	0	0	70	0	30	0	0
Gross Domestic Product at Purchaser's Value (million US$)	3300	1025	208	1343	2360	372	5232	3428	6545
Gross National Product or Private Consumption Expenditures per Head (US$)	.470	702	220	173	n.a.	425	209	330	577

Source: Food and Agriculture Organization of the United Nations, *Fishery Country Profiles* (Rome: FAO, 1983).

Botswana

Botswana is landlocked, but produces 200-350 tons of fish from Lake Ngami on a subsistence basis. At the national level fish contributes little to the animal protein supply, but it is important in the drought-stricken north-west where livestock production is limited by the presence of the tsetse fly. The people of Botswana consume little fish, but there are no significant cultural inhibitions against it. The Department of Food Resources distributes dried fish to schools and clinics. More than half the fish supply is imported, mainly from South Africa.

Lesotho

While there is some pond production, fish is only of minor importance in landlocked Lesotho. Most fish consumed is imported marine fish in frozen or canned form. Fish makes only a small contribution to the diet.

Malawi

The main source of fish production in Malawi is Lake Malawi, which is shared with Mozambique and Tanzania. Other lakes also serve as important sources of fish, but all have highly variable yields. Most of the catch is used for domestic consumption, whether fresh, sun-dried, or smoked. The price of fish is lower than that of meat in most areas, but it tends to be scarce and expensive in the northern and central regions, away from the productive southern sections of Lake Malawi.

For most Malawians, fish represents the principal source of animal protein, accounting for more than 60 percent of animal protein intake. Ground maize is the staple food, with the result that protein deficiency is a serious problem. Infant mortality levels are very high. The government is trying to increase protein availability in the rural communities, and it is giving high priority to the production of fish.

116

Imports of fish are small, most for the tourist industry. A small amount of fish is exported to neighboring Zambia and Zimbabwe. There might be good potential for increasing production, especially from Lake Malawi.

Mozambique

Marine fisheries account for more than 90 percent of Mozambique's production. Shrimp exports, primarily to Japan, account for about 20 percent of the country's foreign exchange earnings. Shrimp and some pelagic fish are produced by joint ventures with Spain, Japan, and the Soviet Union. Most of the by-catch from the shrimp operations--about 20,000 to 30,000 tons annually--is discarded at sea.

Pelagic species landed along the coast are consumed mainly in the coastal areas. Lake-based inland fisheries, which supply inland areas, have considerable underutilized potential. The inadequate development of small-scale fisheries to supply local demand was demonstrated by the importation in 1981 of about 13,000 pounds of fish for local consumption.

Mozambique has very high potential production, but in the short-term it cannot be utilized because of its political problems.

Swaziland

With only two main rivers, landlocked Swaziland does not have a tradition of fish production or consumption. Most fish consumed is imported either frozen or canned for higher income groups in urban areas. There is some potential for increasing fish production from lakes and reservoirs.

Tanzania

Marine and lake fisheries in Tanzania yield a substantial supply of fish, but production could be increased with suitable development measures. Most of the fish is consumed fresh near the production sites, but smoked and dried fish is transported over wider areas, and some is exported to neighboring countries. Consumers prefer freshwater fish, particularly the dried "dagaa" which is produced from *Stolothrissa tanganica* and *Limnothrissa miodon* and other very small fish. Smoked tilapia and other freshwater fish are also popular. Some shrimp is exported to Japan and to Europe, some goes to hotels and restaurants in Dar-es-Salaam, and some is dried for domestic consumption.

Fish is important in the Tanzanian diet, accounting for about 30 percent of the animal protein supply, but its distribution within the country is very uneven, partly because of transportation difficulties.

Better use could be made of the fisheries resources of Lake Victoria, particularly the haplochromis. The Tanzanian Food and Nutrition Center together with the Nyegezi Fisheries Training Institute in Mwanza have worked on distributing fresh haplochromis, iced in insulated boxes, and efforts have been made to produce dried and minced haplochromis as well. In the 1970s an unsuccessful attempt was made to produce fish protein concentrate from haplochromis.

Zambia

Zambia's inland fish resources are exploited very vigorously, drawing not only on lakes and rivers but also on dams and ponds. Local production is augmented by imports of fish from Tanzania. Fish constitutes a major source of animal protein in the Zambian diet, but local supply is not adequate to meet the demand.

Zimbabwe

Almost half of landlocked Zimbabwe's fisheries production is from Lake Kariba in large-scale, capital-intensive operations. Stocked reservoirs also yield considerable quantities of fish. More than 80 percent of the catch is brined and sundried, with the rest being sold frozen or used as food in crocodile farms along the lake. Demand for fish is strong, requiring imports of several thousand metric tons each year, but imports are limited because of the inadequate supply of foreign exchange.

NUTRITION SITUATION

A 1984 study on *SADCC Agriculture: Toward 2000* analyzing the situation and alternative futures found that all nine SADCC countries have significant problems of malnutrition, and seven of them--Angola, Botswana, Lesotho, Mozambique, Tanzania, Zambia, and Zimbabwe-- faced exceptional food shortages in both 1983 and 1984.[2] The study concluded that "a continuation of past trends spells disaster," but with "improved performance" or with "high performance" food self-sufficiency would increase.

The study acknowledged that "both marine and in-land fisheries are important for SADCC countries in pro-viding employment, foreign exchange and above all a basic component of national diets." It noted the substantial un-derutilized potential in fisheries production, and suggested specific interventions in the provision of fishing gear and in the integrated development of artisanal fisheries. The study also suggested regional cooperation in the de-velopment of fishery resources shared by SADCC coun-tries such as those in Lake Malawi and Lake Kariba, or between SADCC countries and other neighboring countries such as those in Lake Victoria and in Lake Tanganyika.

Food production per capita in the SADCC countries in 1982-84 averaged only 81 percent of what it was in 1972-74. This is far below the figure of 116 percent for all low income countries, and well below the average of 92 percent for the countries of sub-Saharan Africa.[3] Agricultural crop yields have stagnated and declined. The region imports large quantities of food, particularly of wheat and rice, which represents a shift away from traditional, locally-produced staples.

Table 8.2 shows the quality of the overall diet and the role of fish in it. South Africa is included for pur-poses of comparison. Table 8.3 shows how the supply of fish for consumption is affected by the pattern of production, imports, and exports in the SADCC countries. Although the data, being recent, should be regarded as tentative, it is clear that nutrition in the SADCC countries could be improved considerably. It is also clear that the per capita supply of fish is quite low in some of the SADCC countries. It is below the world average of 12.3 kg/year even in the three coastal countries.

The data in Tables 8.2 and 8.3 do not convey the degree to which the distribution of resources may be skewed. In Tanzania, for example, "Whilst those people living at or near the coast or lakeshore may be consuming as much as 80 kg per head per year, those in the central zones get virtually none. It follows that any attempts to raise per capita consumption of fish through increased consumption must be matched by parallel, concurrent efforts to improve distribution."[4]

OPTIONS

The low level of consumption of fisheries products in the SADCC countries suggests that there are good possibilities for increasing the use of fish in the region. There are important cultural constraints against eating fish among some groups, but the inadequate income is probably the more important limiting factor. Many Africans do not have enough money to purchase as much fish as they would like.

Surely the most desirable way to increase consumption by the poor is to increase their incomes so they are no longer poor. However, until that broader development objective can be fulfilled, many different things could be done in the supply, processing, and distribution phases of fisheries activities to increase consumption within the existing constraints of limited incomes.

Supply

The supply of fishery products available for consumption in the SADCC region could be increased, in

TABLE 8.2

Per Capita Food Supply, 1982-84

	Ango-la	Bot-swana	Les-tho	Mala-wi	Mozam-bique	Swazi-land	Tan-zania	Zam-bia	Zim-babwe	South Africa
GRAND TOTAL										
Quantity per year (kilograms)	471	384	407	479	393	432	684	359	301	564
Quantity per day (grams)	1292	1051	1116	1313	1077	1184	1874	983	826	1545
Energy per day (calories)	1975	2076	2349	2417	1687	2548	2296	1968	1887	2946
Protein per day (grams)	43	65	69	69	29	62	52	53	47	77
ANIMAL PRODUCTS										
Quantity per year (kilograms)	60	116	67	25	20	101	51	40	37	130

Quantity per day (grams)	163	317	184	69	54	278	139	109	100	357
Energy per day (calories)	183	345	172	91	57	332	144	124	142	429
Protein per day (grams)	13	22	13	6	4	22	11	11	9	28

FISH AND SEAFOOD

Quantity per year (kilograms)	8	2	3	9	4	.1	12	11	2	10
Quantity per day (grams)	22	6	8	25	11	.2	32	30	6	27
Energy per day (calories)	20	4	6	17	8	---	21	20	4	1
Protein per day (grams)	3	.7	1	3	1	---	3	3	.6	3

Note: These data should be regarded as provisional.

Source: Food and Agriculture Organization of the United Nations.

Table 8.3

PROVISIONAL FOOD BALANCES FOR
FISH AND FISHERY PRODUCTS, 1980-82

	Ango-la	Bot-swana	Leso-tho	Mala-wi	Mozam-bique	Swazi-land	Tan-zania	Zam-bia	Zim-babwe
Production (1000 mt live weight)	110	1.4	.019	58.5	39	.044	228	48	16
Non-food uses (1000 mt live weight)	37.8	0	0	0	0	0	254	0	0
Imports (1000 mt live weight)	15	457	4.9	.7	10	0	.9	5.8	2
Exports (1000 mt live weight)	13.8	10	0	6	4.6	0	.4	1	74
Food supply (1000 mt live weight)	73	1.8	4.9	53	44.6	.44	229	54	17.8
Population (millions)	7.9	.9	1.4	6	12.5	.57	19.5	5.8	7.6
Per capita supply (kg/year)	9.2	1.9	3.6	8.6	3.6	0.1	11.7	9.3	2.3

Source: Food and Agriculture Organization of the United Nations, *1984 Yearbook of Fishery Statistics: Fishery Commodities*, Vol. 59 (Rome: FAO, 1986), p. 254.

principle, by increasing production, by increasing imports, by reducing exports, or by decreasing wastes.

As indicated in the bottom row of Table 8.4, there is great potential for increasing fisheries production in the SADCC countries. In the cases of Angola and Mozambique, however, development of these resources probably could not be undertaken until political stability is restored.

In 1982 catches by foreign fleets in marine waters were more than double those of the SADCC countries. As Table 8.4 shows, a very large share of the marine catch is not landed locally, but is taken elsewhere by foreign-flag vessels. There is no prospect that African-flag vessels could replace the foreign fishing vessels in the short term. Moreover, even if African vessels were to control a larger share of the fisheries, it might still be wise to land the catch of high-value products elsewhere.

The local landings of fish by foreign-flag vessels are categorized as imports, even if the fish came from African waters. The local landings generally consist of frozen blocks of those whole fish which remain after the vessels have selected out the high-value species. The frozen blocks are moved inland to some extent, and the fish are dried and smoked after they are thawed. Since it is essentially a spinoff product, incidental to the vessels' major operations targeted on the higher value species, the fish landed in African ports is very inexpensive, sometimes as low as US$300/ton. Thus in future contract negotiations for access by these foreign vessels it might be wise to press for larger quantities of these "imports."

Local supplies could also be increased by reducing wastes, particularly by making better use of the by-catches associated with shrimp operations. Improved handling and processing in small-scale traditional could reduce waste by reducing spoilage. However, while reducing wastes could increase the overall supply available for local consumption, it may not increase the supply of inexpensive products available for the poor.

In inland fisheries, the engineering requirements for adapting reservoirs to fish production are being given increasing attention.[5] The production of fish in irrigation facilities also can be greatly enhanced if that prospect is

TABLE 8.4

1982 Catches and Potential
('000 metric tons)

	Ango-la	Bot-swana	Les-tho	Mala-wi	Mozam-bique	Swazi-land	Tan-zania	Zam-bia	Zim-babwe
Total Local Catch	136	1.4	.02	51	35.5	.15	226	62	15
Total Catch, Local and Foreign	535	1.4	.02	51	52	.15	226	62	15
Marine Potential	655	---	---	---	85	---	40	---	---
Inland Potential	113	24	.29	150	55	.2	297	270	22
Total Potential	768	24	.29	150	140	.2	337	---	---
Difference Between Potential and Catch	233	22.6	.27	99	87	.05	111	208	7

Source: Southern African Development Coordination Conference, SADCC Agriculture: Toward 2000 (Rome: Food and Agriculture Organization of the United Nations, 1984), p. 4.2.

taken into account in the design stage, but that potential is often neglected.[6] Extensive planning for aquaculture development is underway.[7] It would be useful to give more explicit attention to the nutritional dimension of these activities.

Inland fisheries have a great volume of under-utilized potential in the SADCC countries. Moreover, for any given volume of new production they are likely to contribute more to the alleviation of malnutrition than marine fisheries because they are more likely to be located in areas of low fish consumption, they are less likely to produce species for export, they tend to require less capital, and they are more directly accessible by the poor. In reference to Tanzania, for example, it has been observed that "the real influence of even smaller reservoirs in nutritionally deprived areas can be out of all proportion to the size of the water and as much as possible should be done to encourage the development of such small-scale fisheries."[8]

Processing

Dried and smoked fish are inexpensive and very popular in Africa. Improvements in these already familiar techniques to increase shelf life and reduce insect infestation could yield substantial benefits. Improved preservation techniques should be developed in areas that suffer periodic gluts and shortfalls in supply. Better storage and transport containers could be helpful as well. However, care should be taken to not improve the product so much that it becomes unavailable to the poor.

Distribution

It is important to assure not only the production of suitable low-cost products but also an effective marketing chain reaching from the suppliers to those most vulnerable to malnutrition, especially in remote areas. Adequate means should be provided for handling, storage, and transportation. Pricing patterns should assure that a good balance is found between providing adequate incentives to producers and modest prices for poor consumers. The share of profits captured by middlemen should be in line with the value of the services they provide.

Fish is used in institutional feeding programs in Botswana where salted, sun-dried fish is included in the government's Direct Food Assistance Programme. The Department of Food Resources buys the dried, salted fish directly from the fishermen for redistribution to schools, clinics, and other institutions. While providing relief from malnutrition, the program also supports fishermen by providing them with a ready market and guaranteed prices for their products. This sort of non-market distribution of fisheries products could be expanded in all of the SADCC countries.

Increasing fisheries trade among the SADCC countries could contribute to the alleviation of malnutrition, but there are risks and difficulties. As shown earlier, in Chapter 2, trade tends to move fisheries products from poorer people to richer people. If the flow of income in the opposite direction does not reach the poor, or if it is not used to purchase the basic food that is needed, increasing trade can lead to reduced food supplies for the poor.[9]

The situation can be especially problematic where local fisheries production, processing, and marketing are dominated by foreign interests through joint ventures or other mechanisms. The poor country which hosts such operations may retain only a small share of the benefits. For example, Namibia, whose fisheries operations are largely controlled by South African interests, gets little benefit from those operations.[10]

One major impediment to increasing trade within the region is that the present transportation infrastructure was developed primarily for transportation to ports and thus to and from industrialized market economies outside Africa. Many transportation routes of the SADCC countries have been directed toward South Africa. The Southern Africa Transport and Communications Commission (SATCC, of SADCC) is addressing this issue as part of its overall effort to strengthen transport and communication facilities among SADCC countries. One of its major projects is to restore a railway line to provide Malawi with access to the Mozambican port of Nacala.

Another problem is that there is a scarcity of foreign exchange in the SADCC countries. To an extent this problem might be overcome through "countertrade," the bartering of goods in kind.

The most serious issue is that developing African countries simply are not yet strong markets for fisheries products, either in the quantities they demand or in the prices they can offer. However, the terms of trade with developed countries often are unfavorable for developing countries, and in many cases they are deteriorating. Proposals for increasing regional trade should be evaluated not only in narrow commercial terms but also with respect to their potential impact on local nutritional status, food security, the distribution of benefits within the region, and the reduction of dependency on developed countries. Developed countries might offer higher prices for specific fisheries products, but it should be recognized that for trade between African countries, the benefits from both ends of the transaction remain within the continent.

Although its value cannot be measured in economic terms, increasing trade among nations of the region could build up solidarity among them, enhancing their political and economic power, both individually and collectively.

The export of high value products such as shrimp from the region probably should continue because of their important contribution to foreign exchange earnings and because that income allows for the purchase of basic foods. In expanding trade within the region, some products such as Nile perch might be more likely to go to the hotel trade. Other products such as kapenta, dagaa, and haplochromis would be more likely to go to people at risk of malnutrition. Of course it should be assured that such products are shipped only from areas of excess supply. A careful study would have to be made to determine whether that sort of trade would be economically sustainable, or if it would warrant some sort of subsidy.

ACTION

Several lines of action could be taken to enhance the contribution of fisheries to the alleviation of malnutrition in southern Africa. SADCC could support separate national actions and could facilitate activities of broad regional interest.

Promoting Regional Trade

SADCC could help to promote regional trade in fisheries products by providing appropriate market intelligence. This function could be carried out on a continuing basis by one of the national fisheries departments or by a new body created for the purpose. The service could be provided on a regional basis in collaboration with FAO's INFOPECHE Marketing Information Service in Abidjan, Ivory Coast. It should also be coordinated with SADCC's food security project on regional food marketing infrastructure, and with the PTA organization (Preferential Trade Area for Eastern and Southern African States) headquartered in Lusaka.

SADCC Agriculture: Toward 2000 concluded its chapter on regional cooperation by saying that the regional trade and marketing centers for fish could serve as models for a marketing service covering food in general. Drawing on the experience of the FAO Fish Marketing Information System in Abidjan and throughout the world, a new body could take the lead in promoting overall SADCC regional trade.

Before any permanent arrangements are made a study should be done to determine if the prospects for increased regional trade in fisheries products are in fact promising. Current imports into the region and the continent should be reviewed to determine whether they could be replaced with local products. In some cases this continental import substitution might require investment in processing facilities. Existing and potential production would have to be surveyed and the character of the markets would have to be estimated. Facilities for marketing, such as transportation and storage facilities, financial arrangements, and quality control measures would have to be assessed as well.

Small Pelagics

There is great potential for increased production of small pelagics such as kapenta and dagaa from inland waters in the region, and there is great demand for them, especially in dried, smoked, and salted forms. Understanding of their production, handling, and use is already well advanced in the region, so that communities which have great familiarity with, say, storage, could share their experience with others.

Good research has already been launched by FAO's Committee for Inland Fisheries of Africa (CIFA) and others on the small pelagics, but that research has emphasized issues of production.[11] If planning for a regional program is to be based on a sound foundation, a descriptive study should be made of the entire system of production, processing, and distribution of small pelagics, with careful attention given to patterns of consumption as well. With that as a base, potentials for improved usage could be systematically investigated, identifying suitable programs of action at both the national and regional levels.

Fisheries Policy and Programs

In several SADCC countries the stated objectives of fisheries development do not explicitly include nutritional considerations. They should adopt as official policy that one of the objectives is to enhance the contribution of fisheries to the alleviation of malnutrition. Then, possibly with FAO assistance, the countries could formulate specific programs of action. Even before full programs are designed, fisheries development projects which are still in the planning stages or are already underway should be systematically reviewed to determine if their nutritional impacts could be improved.

SADCC could coordinate a regional program on small pelagics (or on trade), possibly involving not only the SADCC countries but also other developing African countries. Several of the SADCC fisheries projects already proposed could be drawn together under the program to form a unified whole. In taking a regional overview SADCC could help to match areas of surplus supplies with areas of deficiency, and advise regarding suitable means of transport and handling. It could advise international agencies such as the World Food Programme regarding suitable sources of supply. It could develop appropriate quality standards. This facilitation work could be of great service to producers as well as to consumers. Moreover, a regional project to help increase the use of fish in alleviating malnutrition would help to fulfill SADCC's fundamental objectives in that it could reduce economic dependence, strengthen regional integration, mobilize underutilized resources, and provide a sound basis for cooperation among the SADCC countries.

NOTES

1. Full country profiles may be found in *Africa South of the Sahara 1986*, Fifteenth edition (London: Europa Publications, 1985).
2. Southern African Development Coordination Conference, *SADCC Agriculture: Toward 2000* (Rome: Food and Agriculture Organization of the United Nations, 1984).
3. World Bank, *World Development Report 1986* (New York: Oxford University Press, 1986), p. 190.
4. *A Framework for the Formulation and Implementation of a National Fishery Policy in Tanzania* (Rome: FAO/ Norway Cooperative Programme, 1984).
5. C. H. Clay, *New Reservoirs in Africa, 1980-2000* (Rome: FAO CIFA Occasional Paper No. 11, 1984); J. M. Kapetsky and T. Petr, *Status of*

African Reservoir Fisheries (Rome: FAO CIFA Technical Paper No. 10, 1984); C. J. Vanderpuye, *Evaluation Guidelines for Rational Planning and Management of Tropical and Subtropical Inland Fisheries Under Constraints from Other Uses of Land and Water Resources: Africa* (Rome: FAO Fisheries Circular No. 789, 1985).

6. *Irrigation in Africa South of the Sahara* (Rome: FAO Investment Center Technical Paper 5, 1986).

7. André Coche and Francois Demoulin, *Report of the Workshop on Aquaculture Planning in the Southern African Development Coordination (SADCC) Countries* (Rome: FAO CIFA Technical Paper No. 15, 1986); *Rural Fishculture Development and Technology Transfer in Eastern and Southern Africa* (Rome: Economic Commission for Africa and FAO, 1985).

8. Food and Agriculture Organization of the United Nations, *A Framework for the Formulation and Implementation of a National Fishery Policy in Tanzania* (Rome: FAO/Norway Cooperative Programme, 1984).

9. Prospects for increasing trade in food commodities other than fish are analyzed in Ulrich Koester, *Regional Cooperation to Improve Food Security in Southern and Eastern African Countries* (Washington, D.C.: International Food Policy Research Institute, 1986). The study examines the likely effects of increased trade on food security (in the sense of stabilizing overall food supplies), but does not examine its likely effect on the incidence of malnutrition.

10. Richard Moorsom, *Exploiting the Sea* (London: The Catholic Institute for International Relations, 1984).

11. See, for example, B. E. Marshall, *Small Pelagic Fishes and Fisheries in African Inland Waters* (Rome: CIFA Technical Paper No. 14, 1984).

Chapter 9

THE PACIFIC ISLANDS

MALNUTRITION

There are serious problems of malnutrition in the Pacific islands. Although absolute food shortages are rare, malnutrition problems occur in all of the Pacific island nations. Infants and children are particularly vulnerable to undernutrition. Recent estimates of infant mortality rates, provided in Table 9.1, suggest that there is very substantial malnutrition in some of the islands. Even where infant mortality rates are moderate, in many islands there are high and increasing rates of diabetes, high blood pressure, dental caries, obesity, and heart disease.[1]

Certain kinds of malnutrition have become more widespread in the Pacific islands as a result of modernization or, as it is sometimes called, westernization or urbanization.[2] However, the causal linkages are not always the same. The seriousness of the problem is not entirely clear either.

Modernization typically involves a complex cluster of phenomena including monetization, urbanization, increased salaried employment, economic growth, population growth, the decline of community and the rise of individual wealth accumulation. Which particular aspects of modernization lead to changes in diet? Is it the increasing availability of money? the lack of sufficient money for food in some urban families? population density? urban life styles? the emphasis on cash cropping? the decline of breastfeeding? the fact that imported foods are often cheaper than indigenous foods? the

TABLE 9.1

Infant Mortality and Life Expectancy

Country	Infant Mortality	Life Expectancy
MELANESIA		
Papua New Guinea	77	50
Fiji		
(Fijians)	30	64
(Indians)	41	62
Solomon Islands	53	54
Vanuatu	94	55
New Caledonia		
(Melanesians)	39	60
(Europeans)	9	73
POLYNESIA		
Western Samoa	33	63
French Polynesia	57	62
Tonga	41	63
American Samoa	18	70
Cook Islands	29	67
Wallis & Futuna	49	63
Tuvalu	43	59
Niue	11	67
Tokelau	37	n.a.
MICRONESIA		
Guam	13	73
Fed. States of Mic.	45	58
Kiribati	93	52
Marshall Islands	45	60
N. Marianas Islands	26	66
Palau	28	66
Nauru	31	55

Source: R. Taylor, N. Lewis, and S. Levy, *Mortality in Pacific Islands Countries--A Review Circa 1980* (Noumea: South Pacific Commission, 1986).

prestige value of processed and imported foods? the convenience of processed foods? In the 1950s it was already being reported that "bread and sugar were regularly consumed by villagers engaged in subsistence agriculture on Rarotonga. The average family was consuming 1535 grams of white bread and 106 grams of sugar per day."[3] How can we understand this? How does modernization lead to changes in diets?

Modernization certainly is associated with changes in diets, but is that change always for the worse? The data show great increases in "diseases of civilization" such as diabetes, high blood pressure, heart disease and problems associated with improper use of infant formula. But the modernization of diets and other aspects of lifestyle probably has also led to the decline of some more "traditional" health problems such as infectious diseases. Certainly infant mortality rates have declined and life expectancies have increased with modernization. Referring to the people of Bougainville in Papua New Guinea, Douglas Oliver judges that:

> Despite the predictions of some experts, the partial or in some cases total changeover to store-bought foods has not resulted in an overall deterioration in health--on the contrary, the increased protein content of some of these foods has had nutritionally beneficial effects.[4]

Traditional diets have been generally sound, but some specific practices were not. For example, the avoidance of green leafy vegetables or of ripe papaya has often led to unnecessary vitamin deficiencies.[5] In some cultures small children are fed last, making them particularly vulnerable to malnutrition.[6]

If we compare the more traditional with the more modern island societies today, we could not by any means argue that the traditional societies enjoy better general health. There have been some traditional forms of malnutrition, still observable in the more remote areas. Modernization does not introduce malnutrition; it exchanges old forms for new forms.

There is a tendency to romanticize traditional ways and to suggest that all of the ills of island societies were introduced by the colonists. To describe modernization (or westernization, or urbanization) as the root of malnutrition in the islands is much too simplistic, and it is not helpful. What exactly is it about modernization that needs to be managed better?

In my view, modern malnutrition in the Pacific is largely due to the fact that islanders are losing control over their own diets. The increasing availability of money and thus of store goods--particularly imports--certainly increases the range of choice, at least for those who can afford the products. But the process also enlarges the islanders' vulnerability to alien influences in the formation of their choices from this rich variety.

This outside influence, whether from local store operators or from foreign corporations, is not neutral and it is not designed to promote good nutrition. The business of these outsiders is business. It happens that the more profitable commercial foods often are less nutritious than traditional foods. Local merchants promote soft drinks rather than coconut milk only because selling soft drinks normally is more profitable.

Similarly, food products such as white bread, doughnuts, and biscuits (cookies) are promoted locally because of the profits they can yield, not because of their nutritive value. Wheat products generally go to those with money, especially in the urban centers. To the extent that they are consumed by the poor, as prestige foods, they tend to displace other more highly nutritive foods which could be obtained at lower cost. The Pacific islands, like other developing nations, have enormously increased their imports of wheat in recent years, not so much because of real needs but because of the vigor with which wheat is marketed by the exporting nations. The dangers of the wheat addiction have already been recognized elsewhere.[7]

Increasingly, patterns of production are oriented toward accommodating outside interests. Some development plans give little attention to the production of food for local consumption. In the Marshall Islands, for example, if livestock is excluded, the agriculture budget for local food production amounts to 0.15 percent of the overall budget for 1985-1989.[8]   This inattention to production for local consumption is indicated by the data of Table 9.2. Of the nations listed, significant gains in local food production per capita have been achieved only in the Solomon Islands, while in the others there has been little or no gain. Even more significantly, in many of the island nations the productivity varies sharply over time, suggesting considerable insecurity in food supplies.

The market orientation introduces pressures into the islands which lead to deterioration in the quality of nutrition. This is an empirically observed tendency, not a logical necessity. People can be empowered to regain control over their diets. In Yap, for example, the increasing consumption of Coca Cola was reversed with a campaign based on the slogan, "Things go better with coconuts." Empowerment arose through a form of education which went beyond comparison of the nutrients in the two products. In this instance nutrition education also entailed helping people to understand why Coca Cola was promoted so vigorously and whose interests it served. Thus nutrition education can become a form of political education. It can become a means of empowerment, helping people to gain increasing control over their own diets, to serve their individual and community interests.[9]

FOOD TRADE

Modern malnutrition in the Pacific appears to be associated with the pattern of trade that has emerged. Although highly self sufficient in the past, the islands now import a very large share of their food. In the early 1960s Fiji's food import bill already amounted to about 25 percent of the income derived from the export of agricultural products[10] In 1975 Fiji's food imports accounted for 19 percent of all imports.[11] By 1976 Funafuti, the main atoll of Tuvalu, imported 80 percent of its total food needs.[12] In the early 1950s food accounted for less than 10 percent of the value of imports in Tonga, but that figure moved up to over 30 percent by the early 1970s.[13] In 1982 fully half of the value of consumer goods

Table 9.2

Index of Food Production Per Capita
(1974-76 = 100)

	1973	1974	1975	1976	1977	1978	1979	1980	1981	1982	1983
Cook Islands											
	101	83	106	111	113	98	64	90	83	92	104
Fiji											
	112	102	98	100	110	111	139	121	132	134	92
Papua New Guinea											
	99	100	101	100	98	97	97	96	95	97	97
Western Samoa											
	98	98	100	102	105	101	100	101	104	103	100
Solomon Islands											
	92	100	97	102	113	116	126	120	132	129	138
Tonga											
	88	93	103	104	98	91	90	96	101	86	86
Vanuatu											
	81	105	98	97	93	106	107	81	99	82	82

Source: *Statistical Yearbook for Asia and the Pacific* (Bangkok, Thailand: Economic Commission for Asia and the Pacific, 1985).

imported into the Marshall Islands consisted of food, beverages, and tobacco.[14]

The islands are highly dependent on imported food, but that does not mean that they should try to move to the other extreme and import no food at all. Large continental nations such as the United States import great quantities of food. Insistence on total self sufficiency for small island nations would mean sacrificing the very considerable benefits which could be obtained from engaging in trade. Trade can bring in some products at lower cost than they can be produced domestically. It provides for greater variety and often higher quality foods. And engagement in trade can enhance food security by providing access to food supplies in times of local shortfalls. However, high dependency on imported food also means that the islands have low food security in that they are vulnerable to cut-offs when food supplies become short elsewhere in the world.[15] More importantly, with a declining capacity for self-provisioning, their bargaining power is reduced, and they become compelled to accept unfavorable prices. That is already clearly the pattern for their exports.

Outside nations with greater bargaining power derive substantial benefits from trade with the Pacific islands. Thus they promote a level of dependency on trade which goes well beyond that warranted in terms of the islanders' own self interests. The large-scale imports of junk food demonstrate this pattern very clearly.

The Pacific islands need to be discriminating and ask how much of which kinds of food should be exported or imported, under what sorts of conditions. Their task is to find a middle way. Surely some high value food products such as tuna or ginger or vanilla should be exported, although care is required to assure that the benefits flow properly and to assure that environmental damage is kept in check. Some foods, such as rice, sensibly should be imported because they yield substantial nutritive value at modest cost and have few local substitutes. However, even rice imports can be excessive. Careful analyses need to be made on a commodity by commodity basis, taking into account not only economic but also nutritional impacts.

THE FISHERIES SITUATION

Resource Potential

Most of the Pacific ocean is comprised of very deep water, with substantial continental shelves found only off Papua New Guinea. Conditions in the tropical Pacific as a whole are such that phytoplankton and zooplankton densities are low, and thus the fish stocks in the region also are sparsely distributed.

Several major stocks of tuna migrate through the Pacific region, with seasonal variations in their migration patterns. Tuna is the major commercial fisheries resource in the region. Prior to the extension of jurisdiction over fisheries resources out to 200 nautical miles in the late 1970s and early 1980s, the offshore waters of the islands were heavily exploited by vessels of distant-water fishing nations, primarily by Japan, Korea, and Taiwan. Access is now provided through licensing arrangements on a fee basis, and also through joint venture arrangements. There is considerable poaching.

Whale consumption has declined sharply because of depleted stocks, reduced demand, restrictions imposed by the International Whaling Commission, and pressures imposed by environmental organizations such as Greenpeace.

Dolphins, dugong, and turtles are not harvested commercially, but they are used on a subsistence basis in some areas.

In Papua New Guinea there are substantial freshwater fish resources. Tilapia, deliberately introduced in the 1950s, has become an important source of animal protein in some regions.[16] Barramundi, which depends on Papua New Guinea's rivers for part of its life cycle, is of significant commercial importance. There is a freshwater clam fishery in Fiji which produces some 700 tons per year. The other less developed Pacific island territories have no significant freshwater fisheries. There are some small freshwater fisheries of localized interest.

The nearshore resources are less abundant than they are near continental landmasses:

The smallness of the landmasses greatly restricts the nutrient run-off available to enrich the surrounding ocean. Therefore, the waters surrounding them are typically clear and blue and, compared to continental coastal areas, of low productivity. As a result of this lack of extensive continental shelf or coastal enrichment, small Island states have limited inshore fish resources and hence restricted new inshore fishery potentials.[17]

Nevertheless, the islands do have appreciable quantities of fish along their ocean shores and in their lagoons.

Local Supplies

Traditionally most fish consumed in the Pacific islands have been marine fish taken from nearshore or lagoon waters. Some forms of aquaculture have been practiced, especially in ancient Hawaii. Milkfish has been cultured in the Cook Islands, Fiji, and Kiribati. In large, high islands, inland "bush" people obtained fish through trade with coastal people. Some freshwater seafoods have been available directly in the highlands, including finfish, mollusks, prawns, and eels. Now much of the fish is caught and distributed on a commercial basis. Fish is sold by roadside vendors and through small village stores as well as through urban markets. In some cases governments provide infrastructure and other support for marketing, as in the case of SIACO, the Solomon Ia (fish) Company, Ltd.

There have been serious shortages of fish available for consumption in the islands, most noticeably in the urban markets:

Tongan waters are a largely untapped source of food, including such fish species as tuna, bill-fish, and shark. In 1973, sale of fish through the Vuna market equaled over $15,000, or 120,000 pounds. However, demand for fish in Nuku'alofa far excelled this amount. Personal observations evidenced that on those days when fish is to be sold, crowds of customers wait hours before the market opens. . . . Despite the fact that domestic demand for fish is unsaturated, 40 percent of the Ekiaki's total catch, for the year 1973, was sent to canneries in Pago-Pago.[18]

In 1978 it was observed that the "demand for fresh fish has never been anything like adequately supplied" in Tonga's capital city of Nuku'alofa.[19] Thaman has noted the "scarce finfish and shellfish in the capital city of Nuku'alofa."[20]

Less obvious to outsiders than the shortages in urban markets is the steadily declining supply from traditional subsistence fisheries:

Local marine foodstuffs (finfish, shellfish, sea urchins, sea slugs, octopi, crustaceans, seaweed, etc.) continue to be critical food resources in coastal areas of large islands and on small islands. However, because of high costs and physical scarcity of fresh marine foods, there is increasing dependence on tinned fish.[21]

The decline in traditional supplies is due not only to the availability of imported fish but also the increasing availability of money, the prestige and convenience of canned fish, the overfishing and exhaustion of some traditional resources, the loss of traditional fishing skills, the lack of supporting infrastructure for local fisheries development, and environmental damage to traditional resources.[22]

Fish Imports

To some extent inadequate local supplies of fish are compensated for with imports. Basic data on fisheries production and trade are provided in Table 9.3. These data probably underestimate production for local consumption, especially that part which is not marketed. A few of the island groups are very large exporters of

TABLE 9.3

Fish Production, Imports, and Exports

I	II	III	IV	V	VI
American Samoa	220	220	636	496	67,979
Cook Islands	n.a.	n.a.	2,876	n.a.	---
Fiji	4,332	11,594	13,380	7,000	4,705
Fr. Polynesia	2,386	2,386	9,650	2,200	---
Kiribati	1,344	1,344	29,263	76	---
Nauru	0	0	10,069	n.a.	---
New Caledonia	499	99	2,357	1,100	121
Niue	20	20	313	50	---
Norfolk Island	n.a.	n.a.	702	---	2
Pap. New Guinea	20,000	8,000	84,845	8,463	20,919
Solomon Islands	1,657	17,444	37,401	150	7,895
Tokelau	n.a.	n.a.	2,095	n.a.	---
Tonga	1,117	1,117	1,951	96	5
T.T.P.I.	4,716	10,000	68,961	n.a.	3,265
Tuvalu	80	80	9,577	n.a.	---
Vanuatu	500	10,500	11,605	930	12,011
Western Samoa	1,700	1,700	1,884	700	---

Key:
I. Country
II. Commercial Catch for Domestic Consumption
    (metric tons)
III. Total Locally Registered Catch (metric tons)
IV. Total Catch from 200-Nautical-Mile Zone (metric tons)
V. Total Import Value (A$'000)
VI. Total Export Value (A$'000)

Source: R. E. Kearney, "Some Economic Aspects of the Development and Management of Fisheries in the Central and Western Pacific," *South Pacific Commission Fisheries Newsletter*, No. 22 (July 1981), pp. 6-15.

fish, while most export only negligible quantities.[23] The islands import large quantities of fish for local consumption, particularly cheap canned mackerel from Japan.[24]

In Fiji in 1970 about two-thirds of the fish consumed was imported canned fish, largely because fresh fish was simply too expensive in the Suva market.[25] In 1974 canned fish imports comprised fully 75 percent of the local fish consumption. In that year Fiji imported F$7,761,000 worth of fish and fish preparations, 18.8 percent of the total value of food imports. Fish has been accounting for a steadily increasing amount and also a steadily increasing proportion of Fiji's food imports.[26] Imports of the most popular canned mackerel, Ocean brand, have been wholly controlled by the Morris Hedstrom company.[27]

In 1971 less than one-tenth of the fish consumed in Western Samoa was locally caught.

In 1978, when the local catch amounted to about 20 tons, Niue imported about 54 tons of fish.

In 1973-74 Papua New Guinea imported almost 22,000 metric tons of canned fishery products, most of it canned mackerel from Japan.

In fiscal 1977 American Samoa imported 2,248,464 pounds of canned fish. This weight was greater than that of every other imported foodstuff except rice. Adding the 737,951 pounds of frozen fish that were imported for local consumption, the total quantity of imported fish was greater than that of any other food item including rice.[28]

In 1974, Yap caught about $2100 worth of fish while importing $550 worth of canned fish, and thus was closer to self sufficiency than any of the other districts of Micronesia. The Marshall Islands, for example, was importing 75 percent of its fish requirements for its urban centers and over 50 percent of its total requirements. Truk produced about $66,500 worth of fish but imported $385,290 worth of canned fish. Palau produced $60,000 of fish but imported $268,287 worth of fish. More recent data on imports of canned fish into Micronesia are provided in Table 9.4. The 1985 total for Yap, 96,179 pounds of imported canned fish, may be compared with the estimated 160,000 pounds of locally caught fresh fish that was sold through stores, restaurants, and institutions

TABLE 9.4

Canned Fish Imports into Micronesia
(pounds)

	Tuna	Mackerel	Sardines
Yap			
1984	18,018	58,516	33,663
1985	21,021	45,244	29,914
Palau			
1984	47,617	58,275	16,170
1985	45,475	55,492	20,244
Truk			
1984	29,137	280,959	22,879
1985	27,982	209,874	17,377
Ponape			
1984	36,435	147,315	52,920
1985	34,818	187,719	62,727
Majuro			
1984	79,065	39,060	48,825
1985	33,127	62,055	26,880
Kosrae			
1984	7,539	31,542	17,335
1985	4,315	19,320	8,820

Source: *Quarterly Report, January-March 1986* (Honolulu: Pacific Fisheries Development Foundation, 1986), p. 23.

in 1985 in Yap. Of course there also are considerable quantities which are not sold, and which are sold but not recorded.

CONFLICTING INTERESTS

The high level of imports of fish and other food to the Pacific islands are of concern because these islands are relatively poor, their economies are fragile, and they show evidence of substantial malnutrition. As one observer from Papua New Guinea asked:

> Why is it that Pacific Island nations are buying large and increasing quantities of meat, fish, dairy products, fruit and vegetables from New Zealand (or from anywhere else for that matter) . . . When fertile countries surrounded by seas that are rich in fish and other seafoods, are importing large quantities of food to supplement their own production (or lack of it), something would appear to be very wrong. . . . The result is that in order to pay for the desired imports the economic resources of the Pacific Island nations are channeled into foreign exchange earning activities and the production for domestic consumption such as food is neglected. Once this happens, there is no choice but to import food, and so the vicious circle goes on. . . . Any nation which promotes a narrow range of export-orientated or foreign exchange earning activities, while notbeing able to feed its own people, becomes particularly vulnerable to outside forces and perpetuates its position as an economic colony. If this state of affairs is judged to be undesirable it is clear that the emphasis must be shifted to boosting domestic production for internal consumption in such vital areas as food production, and at the same time reducing unnecessary imports.[29]

A similar analysis was made by the Regional Fisheries Coordinator for the United Nations Development Programme:

Looking at the region as a whole, I think that one of the most surprising facts that a newcomer learns is that virtually all of the islands rely heavily on imports to meet the demand for fishery products. In many cases, these imports place a relatively heavy drain on the islands foreign exchange reserves, but of even more significance is the recent inflationary trend which is rapidly increasing the price of these commodities. I think that if we were to analyse import data over the past couple of years we would find that these price increases do not directly relate to the increased income of the average islander. Therefore these islands which depend so much on imported fish are facing a situation whereby the per capita consumption of animal protein could be on a downward trend, unless local production can be increased to offset this dependency on imports.[30]

More of Tonga's fish could be exported, but one observer feels that:

In view of the domestic demand for fish products, plus the nutritional status of many urban Tongan inhabitants . . . such exportation would be totally irresponsible to the needs of the Tongan people.[31]

Large quantities of fish are exported from the Pacific islands, mainly tuna which draws a relatively high price on world markets. Most of this fish is caught in large-scale, capital-intensive fishing operations, often in joint ventures with foreign firms, or through the licensing of foreign fishing fleets with no local operations at all. As is evident from national development plans and budgets, fisheries for local consumption have not been promoted nearly as vigorously as export-oriented fisheries. To some extent the export-oriented fisheries have been promoted at the expense of local fisheries.
The historical emphasis on export-oriented fisheries development would not be problematic except for the fact that the benefits returned to the islanders, especially the

148

poorer islanders, have been quite meager.[32] For example, in Fiji,

> . . . there was an attempt to "develop" the fishing industry: i.e. to turn it into an export-oriented enterprise concerned primarily with making profits (mainly for foreign investors) rather than one which emphasized feeding the local population. Accordingly, the Pacific Fishing Company was established with substantial foreign interest and control. . . . The Pacific Fishing Company (PAFCO) is 70% Japanese-owned, with the Fiji government owning 25% of the shares and another 5% available to Fiji residents. . . . While PAFCO has provided profits for its Japanese investors, its contribution to Fiji is debatable. If anything, it has contributed to the country's nutritional problems. About 98% of PAFCO's production is exported. And while in recent years it has contributed over F$10 million in export earnings annually, it has not provided tuna for the local market. Instead, reliance on canned mackerel, imported from Japan at consistently higher prices, has increased.[33]

Similarly, in Vanuatu:

> Fish has become the second largest export item. This export trade is dominated by the South Pacific Fishing Company, part of the Japanese Mitsui group. . . . The company operates a cannery which then ships the fish to Hawaii and elsewhere. Fish is in turn imported, largely from the same Japanese company, and marketed by Burns Philp-owned Keer Brothers. It is a relatively large industry by South Pacific, standards, with most benefits going to foreign companies and a few local bourgeoisie The government itself receives little revenue, only a few locals are employed at relatively low wages and the country's dependency on imported fish is encouraged.[34]

Some fresh tuna is consumed in the islands, but there is also very considerable demand for other species, especially for reef fish which generally are caught by subsistence or small-scale operations. The export fisheries generally do not draw on the same stocks as those fishing for local consumption. The shortages in local supplies are due not so much to the fact that large amounts of tuna are exported as to the fact that fisheries resources suitable for local consumption have been depleted or have not been developed adequately.

The critique of the export-oriented fisheries is not based on the argument that the exported fish would be better used if it were consumed locally. It is based on the observation that the very considerable benefits drawn from the export fisheries do not go to those most in need, and that export fisheries appear to be promoted at the expense of the development of fisheries for local consumption.

One type of conflict of interest is between the Pacific islands and the outside nations involved in their fisheries operations. Outsiders appear to obtain disproportionately large shares of the benefits. One indication of this is that the islands consistently receive less money for their exports than others. For example, in 1979 National Fisheries Development (NFD) of the Solomon Islands was being paid US$472 per ton of skipjack while the standard price, at Terminal Island, California, was US$760. In 1980 NFD was receiving US$487 while the Terminal Island price was US$1200. The gap in prices widens steadily over time, contributing to the overall widening gap in per capita income levels between rich and poor countries.[35]

The second type of conflict is between those at the center and those at the periphery within the Pacific island nations.

Export-oriented fisheries are commonly justified with the explanation that earnings from species which draw a high price on world markets can be used to purchase other inexpensive but nutritious food, and thus meet needs more effectively. This is certainly possible, and it appears to be happening where large quantities of cheap canned mackerel are imported. However, we should ask how all of the the foreign exchange earned from fishing operations is used. It seems evident that little of the income from joint ventures or from licensing fees goes beyond the urban centers to reach the poor or the people on the outer islands--the people most vulnerable to malnutrition.

The failure to support food production for local consumption should not be dismissed as mere neglect by the island governments. People in government apparently see themselves as deriving more benefit--more power-- from increasing tax revenues and from foreign exchange earnings than from having well-nourished populations. The interests of ordinary people, especially those on outlying islands, and those of the major governmental and business groups in the urban centers should not be assumed to be the same.

POTENTIALS

Fisheries development efforts normally place great emphasis on production and give little attention to what becomes of the fish after it is caught. This section reviews the potentials for strengthening fisheries in the Pacific islands specifically for the purpose of alleviating malnutrition.

Production

A prominent expert in Pacific fisheries, Robert Kearney, observes that:

Fish and fisheries have played a central role in the culture, sustenance and recreation of all small island communities. The ability of the traditionally exploited fish resources of the central and western tropical Pacific to continue to provide subsistence protein for island communities is arguably the greatest resource potential of the region, and yet it is one which is commonly overlooked in the quest for more spectacular development options.[36]

Increasing production for local consumption in island fisheries does not necessarily mean reducing fish exports. Some types of fish, as such as the tunas, are too valuable to be reserved for consumption in the islands, and should be exported. The task is not so much to reduce exports as to assure that good supplies of fish are available to those who cannot purchase high priced products in the urban markets.

Nearshore reef and lagoon fisheries resources are over-exploited near the larger population centers in the Pacific islands, but there are considerable under-exploited resources around the less densely populated islands. Even in the currently over-exploited areas, better management might allow recovery and, ultimately, higher yields than have been obtained in the past.[37]   It is also possible to develop fish aggregation devices (FADs) and artificial reefs using materials such as sunken ships or discarded automobile tires.

One major constraint on the development of reef fisheries is the possibility of ciguatera poisoning, which can lead to serious illness in consumers.   The fear of poisoning may be more widespread than is actually warranted.   The toxin is difficult to detect, but detection has been a major focus of scientific research in the region.[38] Several other forms of toxicity (e.g., clupeotoxism) also are matters of serious concern.

There are substantial potentials not only for development of marine resources but also for expansion of freshwater fisheries resources in the high islands.   In Kearney's view, "the socio-economic return from increased yields in these fisheries, particularly in places such as the highlands of Papua New Guinea where animal protein is scarce, could well be relatively much greater than the benefits from similar increases in yields in coastal fisheries where production is relatively higher."

The consensus appears to be that there is little prospect for aquaculture development in the islands, but that assessment is based primarily on consideration of commercial, export-oriented aquaculture.[39]   Traditional aquaculture of the sort practiced historically in Hawaii might be feasible in many of the islands, especially on less heavily populated outer islands.   Milkfish culture,

152

already practiced on several of the islands, might be improved and extended.

A study of the potential for culturing finfish in Fiji led to the observation that "the culture of fish alone may not be economically feasible."

> However, the practice of polyculture of shrimp under extensive operation can be highly profitable. The fish will then constitute a source of relatively cheap protein for local consumption. The shrimp will provide high revenue to farmers and will decrease the import of this item into Fiji and possibly provide a source of foreign currency through export.[40]

Thus fish for local consumption could be produced as a "spinoff product" in which the high priced export-oriented operation in effect subsidizes the product made available for local consumption.[41]

There is good potential for culturing giant clams (*Tridacna gigas*) which "possess an astonishing capability for producing large quantities of edible meat with minimal inputs."[42] Culturing clams is promising not only technically and commercially but also in terms of its potential contribution to local nutrition. The dried adductor muscle can be exported for high prices while the remaining meat, favored in many of the islands, could be made available locally at low cost.[43] The meat that is retained could be viewed as a spinoff product, in effect subsidized by the export of the adductor muscle.

Similarly, trochus is harvested primarily for export (its shell is used for button-making), but the edible flesh is generally underutilized. Although the first temptation may be to explore its commercial potential, explorations might be undertaken into expanding local consumption of the meat, especially on the outer islands.[44]

Processing

Some fisheries resources in the Pacific are available only irregularly, sometimes on a seasonal basis.

Thus there is a need for preservation techniques. Traditional methods such as drying, salting, and smoking can be considerably improved. Canning and freezing generally are too costly for fish destined for local consumption.

Little effort has been invested into improving the ways in which fisheries products are processed for local consumption in the islands. Many years ago a small, simple pamphlet was prepared which described how to salt, dry, smoke, and cook fish in the island context, but it seems to have been forgotten.[45] Improvements in traditional smoking and drying techniques that have been developed elsewhere with the support of agencies such as the Food and Agriculture Organization of the United Nations probably could be adapted to Pacific island contexts.

Since the most serious malnutrition in the islands affects young children, it would be worthwhile to explore methods for improving the use of fisheries products in weaning foods, especially in outer islands where fish may be one of the few good food resources available in abundance.

To improve the use of fisheries products in the alleviation of malnutrition, emphasis should be placed on small-scale local fisheries. However, the potential contribution of large-scale, export-oriented operations should not be ignored. For example, the PAFCO cannery in Fiji produces about 500 metric tons of fishmeal each year.[46] Wastes from such large packing plants might be a good source of organic fertilizer for home gardens. Such spinoff products could be studied to determine if they could be used more effectively for alleviating malnutrition.

Export-oriented tuna catching operations often leave behind substantial quantities of fish unsuitable for canning. This fish has been sold at excessively high prices by Van Camp to local people in Palau.[47] In Majuro, Japanese purse seiners have given away small or damaged tunas to local people. Such practices could hurt local fishermen. These problems might be circumvented if means could be found to systematically channel this fish to those who need it most. Indeed, at the time of negotiating their contracts, export-oriented ventures might be positively obligated to provide fish for selected local nutrition programs. One could also ask canneries to save and encapsulate fish liver oil in areas where there are significant Vitamin A deficiencies.

Distribution

Fish is distributed in the islands through several different mechanisms to reach the consuming family. Usually the most visible form of distribution is commercial marketing, whether that is undertaken through well-organized stores or through small-scale beachfront or roadside vendors. The least visible occurs in subsistence fisheries in which the producer is also the consumer--and thus there is virtually no distribution at all. There also are important patterns of barter and giving of gifts, and in some cases the proceeds of fishing operations are authoritatively allocated by local leaders. These non-commercial means of distribution are of very great importance in the islands. In the Solomon Islands, for example, it was estimated that in 1984 only about 15 percent of the catch for local consumption was traded for cash.[48] There are few institutional feeding programs. In the United States-affiliated territories, for example, school lunches are subsidized with money and commodities from the United States Department of Agriculture. These programs can be used to supply fish to schoolchildren. The USDA school lunch program has provisions requiring that some of the food must be of local origin. If locally caught fish were used, the program could help to promote improved nutrition while at the same time helping to strengthen local fisheries.

Consumption

A great deal could be done to improve the ways in which fisheries products are used after they reach the household. In many of the islands, when only a limited amount of fish is available it is reserved for consumption by adult males and by the elderly. Little fish is consumed by infants, children, and young women--the groups most vulnerable to malnutrition.

Various taboos constraining the use of fisheries should be reviewed. In Kiribati, for example:

> Certain types of fish are forbidden to be eaten. Some parents believe that it is not good to give children fish, it makes them lazy. During local traditional dancing boys and girls are not allowed to eat fish three days before the dancing begins.[49]

However, some traditional beliefs reinforce catching and eating fish:

> In Northern Kiribati children are woken up at night no matter what time, (depending on when the men return from torch fishing) to eat fresh fish. The belief is that if children are fed with fish at all times they will, when grown ups, continue to go fishing to satisfy their demand for fish. However, contrast to this is the Southern Kiribati who believe that if a child is fed with fish at this age, below one and over, will become a beggar for food.[50]

While some taboos have no evident basis in fact, some represent adaptations to very real problems such as the danger of ciguatera poisoning. Such beliefs should be examined carefully before they are dismissed as unreasonable.

Improvements in patterns of consumption may be brought about through programs of education for consumers. However, there is a tendency to focus this education rather narrowly, on fish preparation techniques, for example. It may be useful to broaden educational programs so that they also help people to understand why there are pressures on them to consume foods which are costly and not particularly good for them.

Fisheries Development Planning

If the Pacific islands are to enhance their self-sufficiency with respect to food, fish is certainly one resource in which they have a comparative advantage. However, following the pattern in agriculture, planning for fisheries in the Pacific has provided little support for the development of fisheries for local consumption. For example, a recent fisheries development plan for United States-affiliated territories acknowledges the value of subsistence fisheries, but makes no proposals for strengthening them. The reason given is that "they cannot be developed beyond present levels and are over-exploited in many areas," but perhaps more significantly, "they offer little opportunity for capital investment."[51] The prospects for strengthening local commercial markets are regarded as slim in comparison with the prospects for developing more lucrative export markets.

Proposals are often made for strengthening production of fish for local consumption in five year development plans, in the South Pacific Commission's *Fisheries Newsletter*, and in the work of agencies such as the Pacific Fisheries Development Foundation. However, the nutritional benefit that might be obtained from local fishing has not been an explicit consideration. Although it is obvious that local fisheries make a substantial contribution to local diets, no attention has been given specifically to the potential for fisheries to help in alleviating malnutrition in the islands.

Small-scale fisheries projects do not always contribute to the alleviation of malnutrition. Consider, for example, the Outer Island Fish Development Project planned for the Marshall Islands:

> The objective of this project is to improve the economic situation in the outer islands through increasing incomes and employment in fisheries. It will lead to an increase in the country's fish production and a resultant greater fish supply of fresh fish to urban areas, thus reducing the need for fish imports and promoting the export of fish products. . . . The project provides for the

construction of fish bases with ice making facilities on 24 atolls and islands each with a 45 foot collector vessel capable of holding 10 tons of fish.[52]

Such a project could yield increasing incomes to a few while at the same time reducing the supply of fish to the majority of people on the outer islands. If no special provisions are made, fisheries products generally are likely to move toward people who are better off, whether locally, in urban centers, or in export markets. If fish is to be used to help alleviate malnutrition, there should be some reason to believe that the product will in fact be used that way.[53]

Fisheries for local consumption are not fully developed in the islands partly because projects have been assessed in narrowly economic terms, and thus have had to compete for capital with export-oriented projects serving wealthy outside markets. To illustrate, in the late 1970s a strong market developed in the Papua New Guinea highlands for salted tilapia fillets ("solpis") from the Sepik River.[54] Production was discontinued, however, apparently for economic reasons. If a careful assessment had been made of the product's importance to the protein-short highlanders, it might have been judged worthwhile to continue production, even if it required a small subsidy.

If local nutritional impacts were taken into account along with economic impacts, some projects which previously had not seemed worthwhile might now be seen as yielding very considerable benefits. As the reality of malnutrition in the islands becomes more widely acknowledged, it should be recognized that fisheries in the Pacific islands have substantial potential for helping to alleviate that malnutrition.

158

NOTES

1. Terry Coyne (with editing by Jacqui Badcock and Richard Taylor), *The Effect of Urbanization and Western Diet on the Health of Pacific Island Populations* (Noumea, New Caledonia: South Pacific Commission, 1984).
2. Coyne, *The Effect of Urbanization . . .* ; William Fenton Clark, *Population, Agriculture and Urbanization in the Kingdom of Tonga* (East Lansing, Michigan: Doctoral Dissertation in Geography, Michigan State University, 1975; Ben R. Finney, "Economic Change and Dietary Consequences Among the Tahitians," *Micronesia*, Vol. 2, No. 1 (June 1965), pp. 1-14; Julian Lambert, "The Effect of Urbanization and Western Foods on Infant and Maternal Nutrition in the South Pacific," *Food and Nutrition Bulletin*, Vol. 4, No. 3 (July 1982), pp. 11-13; R. R. Thaman, "Deterioration of Traditional Food Systems, Increasing Malnutrition and Food Dependency in the Pacific Islands," *Journal of Food and Nutrition*, Vol. 39, No. 3 (1982), pp. 109-121; and R. R. Thaman and W. C. Clarke, eds., *Food and National Development in the South Pacific* (Suva, Fiji: University of the South Pacific, 1983).
3. Coyne, *The Effect of Urbanization . . .*, p. 31.
4. Douglas Oliver, *Aspects of Modernization in Bougainville, Papua New Guinea* (Honolulu: Pacific Islands Studies, University of Hawaii, 1981), p. 22.
5. Susan Parkinson, "Nutrition in the South Pacific--Past and Present," *Journal of Food and Nutrition*, Vol. 39, No. 3 (1982), p. 123.
6. Clark, *Population, Agriculture, and Urbanization . . .*, p. 132.
7. Gunilla Andrae and Björn Beckman, *The Wheat Trap: Bread and Underdevelopment in Nigeria* (London: ZED Books, 1985); Alan Garcia Perez, "Peru

Wants an Historic Re-encounter with its Land," *IFDA Dossier*, No. 52 (March/April 1986), pp. 17-28; Omawale, "Kicking the Wheat Habit," *Pan American Health*, Vol. 8, No. 12 (1976), pp. 12-15.

8. Republic of the Marshall Islands, *First Five Year Development Plan, 1985-1989* (Majuro, Marshall Islands: Nitijela Paper No. 1, 1984).

9. John C. Fine, "Progress Toward Tradition," *Oceans*, Vol. 17, No. 6 (November-December 1984), pp. 24-26; Nancy Rody, "Consumerism in Micronesia," *South Pacific Bulletin*, Vol. 28 (1978), pp. 9-14; Nancy Rody, "Things Go Better with Coconuts: Program Strategies in Micronesia," *Journal of Nutrition Education*, Vol. 10, No. 1 (January-March, 1978), pp. 19-22.

10. Coyne, *The Effect of Urbanization . . .*, p. 26.

11. Michael W. P. Baxter, *Food in Fiji: The Produce and Processed Food Distribution Systems* (Canberra: Australian National University, 1980), p. 6.

12. Coyne, *The Effect of Urbanization . . .*, p. 36.

13. Clark, *Population, Agriculture, and Urbanization . . .*, p. 124.

14. Republic of the Marshall Islands, *First Five Year Development Plan, 1985-1989* (Majuro, Marshall Islands: Nitijela Paper No. 1, 1984).

15. Michael P. Hamnett; Russ J. Surber; Denise E. Surber; and Mark T. Denoncour, "Economic Vulnerability in the Pacific," in John Carter. ed., *Pacific Islands Yearbook*, 15th Edition (Sydney: Pacific Publications, 1984).

16. K. Roger Uwate; Peniasi Kunatuba; Baraniko Raobati; and Charles Tenkanai, *A Review of Aquaculture Activities in the Pacific Islands Region* (Honolulu: Pacific Islands Development Program, East-West Center, 1984).

17. R. E. Kearney, "Fishery Potentials in the Tropical Central and Western Pacific," *South Pacific Commission Fisheries Newsletter*, No. 24 (January-March 1983, pp. 20-31.

18. Clark, *Population, Agriculture, and Urbanization . . .*, pp. 111-112.

160

19. E. Hau'ofa, *Corned Beef and Tapioca: A Report on the Food Distribution System in Tonga* (Suva, Fiji: Centre for Applied Studies in Development, University of the South Pacific, 1978).
20. Thaman and Clark, *Food and National Development in the South Pacific*, p. 23.
21. Thaman and Clark, *Food and National Development in the South Pacific*, p. 23.
22. Harry Burnette Hill, *The Use of Nearshore Marine Life as a Food Resource by American Samoans* (Honolulu: Pacific Islands Program Working Papers, 1978); R. E. Johannes, *Words of the Lagoon: Fishing and Marine Lore in the Palau District of Micronesia* (Berkeley: University of California Press, 1981); Norman J. Quinn; Barbara Koji; and Paul Warpeha, *Subsistence Fishing Practices of Papua New Guinea* (Lae, Papua New Guinea: Appropriate Technology Development Institute, 1984).
23. American Samoa does not record purchases of raw tuna for its two canneries as imports, but does record the canned tuna which is shipped out as exports, thus making it appear that it has an extraordinarily good balance of trade.
24. George Kent, *The Politics of Pacific Islands Fisheries* (Boulder, Colorado: Westview Press, 1980), pp. 92-95; R. C. May, *South Pacific Agricultural Survey 1979: Sector Paper on Fisheries* (Manila: Asian Development Bank, 1979), pp. 19-21.
25. C. C. Lindsey, *Fisheries Training in the Region Served by the University of the South Pacific* (Suva, Fiji: University of the South Pacific, 1972), p. A2.
26. Baxter, *Food in Fiji* . . ., pp. 8, 9.
27. Baxter, *Food in Fiji* . . ., p. 170.
28. *Annual Report, Fiscal Year 1977* (Pago Pago: Office of Samoan Information, Government of American Samoa, 1977), p. 81.
29. C. H. Livesey, "Food Imports," *Pacific Islands Monthly*, July 1976, p. 23.
30. E. O. Oswald, *Seventh Technical Meeting on Fisheries* (Noumea, New Caledonia: South Pacific Commission, 1974), p. 33.

31. Clark, *Population, Agriculture, and Urbanization . . .*, p. 112.
32. Kent, *The Politics of Pacific Islands Fisheries*; Sarah K. Meltzoff and Edward S. LiPuma, *A Japanese Fishing Joint Venture: Worker Experience and National Development in the Solomon Islands* (Manila: International Center for Living Aquatic Resources Management, 1983).
33. Michael C. Howard, Nii-K. Plange; Simione Durutalo; and Ron Witton, *The Political Economy of the South Pacific* (Townsville, Australia: James Cook University South East Asian Monograph Series Number 13, 1983), pp. 179-180.
34. Howard, Plange, Durutalo, and Witton, *The Political Economy of the South Pacific*, p. 198.
35. Kent, *The Politics of Pacific Islands Fisheries*; Meltzoff and LiPuma, *A Japanese Fishing Joint Venture . . . .*
36. Kearney, "Fishery Potentials . . . ," p. 20.
37. Johannes, *Words of the Lagoon . . . .*
38. *Expert Committee on Ciguatera, Report of Meeting* (Noumea, New Caledonia: South Pacific Commission, 1981); Yoshitsugi Hokama and James T. Miyahara, "Ciguatera Poisoning: Clinical and Immunological Aspects," *Journal of Toxicology: Toxins Review*, Vol. 5, No. 1 (1986), pp. 25-54; Nancy Davis Lewis, "Ciguatera--Parameters of a Tropical Health Problem," *Human Ecology*, Vol. 12, No. 3 (1984), pp. 253-273; Nancy Davis Lewis, "Ciguatera in the Pacific: Incidence and Implications for Marine Resource Development," in Edward Ragelis, ed., *Seafood Toxins* (Washington, D.C.: American Chemical Society, 1984).
39. Uwate et al., *A Review of Aquaculture Activities . . . .*
40. D. M. Popper, *Fiji Fish Culture* (Rome: Food and Agriculture Organization of the United Nations, 1977), p. 11.
41. George Kent, *National Fishery Policies and the Alleviation of Malnutrition in the Philippines and Thailand* (Rome: FAO Fisheries Circular No. 777, 1984), pp. 18-19.

162

42. G. A. Heslinga and F. E. Perron, "The Status of Giant Clam Mariculture Technology in the Indo-Pacific," *South Pacific Commission Fisheries Newsletter*, No. 24 (January-March 1983), pp. 15-19.

43. John L. Munro, "Giant Clams--Food for the Future," *ICLARM Newsletter*, Vol. 6, No. 1 (January 1983), pp. 3-4.

44. "Tinned Trochus Makes Delicious Dishes," *South Pacific Commission Fisheries Newsletter*, No. 22 (July 1981), p. 16.

45. H. Van Pel, *Fish Preservation Simplified* (Noumea, New Caledonia: South Pacific Commission, [1960].

46. May, *South Pacific Agricultural Survey 1979* . . ., p. 9.

47. Kent, *The Politics of Pacific Islands Fisheries*, p. 142.

48. *Solomon Islands National Development Plan, 1985-1989* (Honiara: Ministry of Economic Planning, 1985), p. 123.

49. Tion Otang, "Nutrition in the Primary School," in *Report on the First Intersectoral National Nutrition Workshop, 13th-17th June 1983* (Tarawa, Kiribati: USP Centre Teaoraereke, 1983).

50. A. Cati, "Nutrition Problems in Kiribati," in *Report on the First Intersectoral National Nutrition Workshop* . . . .

51. AECOS, Inc./Oceanic Resources, Inc., *Central and Western Pacific Regional Fisheries Development Plan, Vol. 4: Regional Plan* (Honolulu: Pacific Basin Development Council, 1983), p. 169.

52. Republic of the Marshall Islands, *First Five Year Development Plan, 1985-1989*, p. 218.

53. Kent, *National Fishery Policies* . . . .

54. Joe Glucksman, "Papua New Guinea's Sepik River Salt Fish Industry," *South Pacific Commission Fisheries Newsletter*, No. 17 (December 1978), pp. 22-28.

PART 3

GUIDELINES

Chapter 10

FISHERIES PROJECT
EVALUATION AND DESIGN

VALUE OF ALLEVIATING MALNUTRITION

Very little is known about the nutritional impacts of fisheries projects. Searching the fisheries literature, one finds many studies about the nutrition of fish but practically none about the nutrition of people.[1] Fisheries surely do make a significant contribution to human nutrition and, more specifically, to the alleviation of malnutrition, especially in Asia and Africa where the needs are so serious. But the contribution of fisheries to the alleviation of malnutrition has not been documented.

One should be careful about assumptions regarding nutritional impacts. One proposal for improving aquaculture operations in a poor Asian country said in regard to nutrition that:

> While the carp produced under the project are relatively high priced species, the increased supply of animal protein foods on the market as a result of the project will make less expensive fish and meats more available at reasonable prices to lower income groups than would be possible without the project.

The outcome could be just the opposite. Increasing attention to the production of high-priced products can result in a diminished supply of food for the poor. In Southeast Asia, many small-scale fishing operations which

166

once provided inexpensive fish for the local poor are now
devoted to catching high-priced shrimp for export. Their
earnings have improved but there is now less fish available for local people. Experience from many countries
through the world shows that increasing overall food supplies in itself does not necessarily lead to the alleviation
of malnutrition. Whether or not fisheries projects help in
this regard should be treated as an empirical question.

There are serious measurement difficulties. Nu-
tritionists have developed good indicators for assessing the
nutritional status of human populations such as the Gomez
scales based on height and weight measurements of children, but there has been little experience in measuring the
nutritional impacts of specific projects or activities. To
try to assess the effects of a fisheries operation in
terms of measurable changes in the heights and weights
of local children over the short term may be to set up a
predictable "failure."

Surrogate measures might be used. The simplest
approach would be to systematically analyze the disposition
of the products. If the consumers of the products of a
fisheries operation are very poor people (possibly identified in reference to the nationally specified poverty line),
rather than people who are well off, it would be reasonable to infer that that operation is helping to alleviate
malnutrition.

The disposition of fisheries products usually is not
obvious. Increasing production in a given area does not
necessarily mean increasing supplies available for consumption in that area. Even small-scale production units
may supply urban centers or export markets, possibly
through middlemen who buy and consolidate the production
of many small operations. In Ecuador, for example,
shrimp produced for export is gathered from a large
number of very small culturing operations.

Or, products may remain in the local area but go to
the local middle class or local elite rather than to those
most in need. They may go to well-fed men rather than
to women and children who have greater needs.

In assessing projects for their effectiveness in alleviating malnutrition one would want to know precisely
that: the extent to which they help in alleviating malnu-

trition. A sharp distinction should be made between increasing the use of fisheries products for human consumption generally and increasing the use of fisheries products for alleviating malnutrition in particular. In terms of public policy, raising energy intakes from 1600 to 2000 calories per day should be valued much more highly than raising intakes from 2600 to 3000 calories a day. Similarly, increasing protein intake should be valued much more highly for cases in which there is an initially low intake.

RELATIONSHIPS TO OTHER VALUES

Fisheries operations--production, processing, or distribution--must be intrinsically gainful or they must be subsidized, or they will not be sustained. In its narrow meaning gainful means economically profitable in the sense that revenues exceed costs. In its broader meaning gainful means that there is a net benefit, whether that benefit is in money, nutrition, employment opportunities, recreational values, or any other values of concern to the operator. Even gleaning shellfish on drying reefs must be gainful to the person doing it, or it will not be done. What is viewed as gainful to one person may not be viewed as gainful by another.

To be more precise, actions are taken not simply when they are gainful, but when they are more gainful than their alternatives. One gleans on the reef or fishes in ponds when there are no better ways to get food.

In speaking of economic profitability it is useful to distinguish between operations which try to *maximize* economic gains and operations which function with *adequate* economic gains. When working with adequate economic gains there may be opportunities to pursue other values as well, such as nutrition, employment, conservation, and community interests. The government-run Kadiwa stores in the Philippines, for example, are not subsidized, but by accepting less than maximum profits they can give particular attention to the needs of the poor, offering them prices which are lower than the normal market prices. The management task in dealing with any such mix of values is one of optimization, taking into account trade-offs among different values. In contrast, maximizing profit, or any other single value, may require sacrificing values on other dimensions.

Activities which are not initially gainful may become gainful if the structure of incentives faced by the operator is altered; that is, if the operator is suitably subsidized. In many cases private enterprises would not find it worthwhile to provide low cost food for the poor, but would do so if some extra incentive were provided. Subsidies may come from national government treasuries or they may come from international agencies, local administrations, or private sources. Subsidizers will have particular values which motivate them, and they will require that operations be gainful from their point of view, in terms of whatever values are of concern to them.

At times non-gainful enterprises can be transformed into gainful enterprises without subsidies. This might be accomplished with some technological innovation, for example. It might also be accomplished with some sort of social innovation. Institutional feeding programs, for example, restructure the situation by consolidating demand. Selling lunches to schoolchildren or soldiers who make individual choices may not be gainful, but selling lunches to managers who decide for them may be gainful. This sort of restructuring of the situation could involve not only changes in scale but also changes in the value considerations which enter into the decisions.

Fisheries operations have been assessed in terms of their economic impacts but not in terms of their nutritional impacts. This has even been true of projects specifically designed for direct nutritional benefits. For example, in one study of tilapia culture in Cavite in the Philippines, the objective was explicitly stated as being both to increase incomes and to provide improved nutrition for the producer, but the activity was systematically assessed only in terms of its economics.[2]

In one project supported by the Asian Development Bank the main objective was to provide fish at fair prices to low income consumers in the northern and northwestern regions of Thailand where per capita consumption of fish is very low. However, the project's viability was estimated only in terms of financial projections. Socioeconomic benefits (such as employment creation, improved credit for fishermen, increased incomes to fishermen, improvement in fisheries technology, and so on) were enumerated, but they were not evaluated and they were not included in a comprehensive accounting along with the financial considerations. Thus the project was systematically appraised in terms of its finances, but not in terms of its primary objective.

In another case, a feasibility study of integrated fish and duck farming, the nutritional productivity of the operation was estimated to be highly positive, and (because of an unusually low egg-laying rate by the ducks) the economics as negative. The study did not then raise the question of whether the nutritional advantages might compensate for the economic disadvantages. The economic analysis alone was taken to be decisive in determining the feasibility of the project.[3] Project appraisal techniques should be broadened to take account of nutritional impacts along with economic impacts.

Fisheries development projects have been assessed primarily on the basis of their capacity to generate revenues, whether the focus is on profits to owners, contributions to gross national product, or foreign exchange earnings. Increasingly, other considerations such as employment generation and environmental values are being taken into account as well, informally if not analytically. Nutritional considerations should also be treated as a significant factor in fisheries project evaluation.

COSTS

At times the value in nutritional terms of a fisheries development project can be assessed only in rather approximate terms. In fresh or processed form fish products often are less costly than alternative sources of animal protein. However, in assessment of food products for nutrition programs, cost is not a simple and straightforward consideration. Food policy analysts sometimes assume that "food quality is measured by the average price paid for calories."[4] The assumption that quality may be equated with price can be misleading in any context; it is certainly misleading when assessing the nutritional value of food. There is little correlation between the nutritional value of fish and its price. Indeed, many low priced fish species have a significantly higher protein content than high priced fish.[5]

Often average prices or central city prices of fish products are high, but areas can be found in which similar products are less costly. Often products appear on the market at a price which could be greatly reduced if large volume institutional demands were established. Often new and less expensive products not currently on the market could be made available for specific nutrition programs, perhaps through the opening of new fisheries, through the development of new manufacturing processes, or through import channels. Moreover, often the market price is not very significant, as in cases in which the poor fish for themselves.

Market prices convey cost per unit weight of fish, but it may be more useful to know cost per unit weight of utilizable protein or of some other aspect of its nutritional quality. To illustrate, in a study done in Thailand a variety of food items were compared in terms of four different bases for calculating the cost of protein.[6] These measures were:

* Protein Efficiency Ratio: The weight gain of the consuming animal divided by its protein intake;

* Biological Value: The proportion of absorbed nitrogen that is retained;

* Net Protein Utilization: The proportion of nitrogen intake that is retained;

* Chemical Score: Comparison with the protein content of a whole egg.

In this study several forms of plant protein scored more highly, but fish proved to be the lowest cost animal protein source on the basis of biological value and on the basis of protein efficiency. Fish was not assessed on the basis of protein efficiency or on the basis of chemical score.

Products used in institutional feeding programs in general and in government subsidized nutrition programs in particular do not have to meet the same criteria as commercial products on the open market since in these cases it is not the consumer who makes the primary purchasing choice. The costs which governments are willing to bear to accomplish their purposes may be very different from the costs which consumers are willing--or able--to bear in making purchases for their own personal purposes.

A product may be highly cost-effective in comparison with alternative products from the point of view of the manager of the institutional feeding program, but that product still may not be viable as a commercial product on the open market. The Nutripak used in the Philippines, for example, might not be commercially viable--partly because the target consumers do not have enough money and partly because they are not much concerned with its nutritional properties--but it may nevertheless be the best choice for the nutrition program.

One can produce inexpensive protein and still not alleviate anyone's malnutrition. The fact that a product is low-cost at some specific point in the production-processing-distribution-consumption chain does not in itself say anything about how it will be used. The preparation of cheap protein may simply mean that middle-class consumers get a better bargain or that sellers get a higher profit margin. Low cost may be a necessary condition, but it is not likely to be a sufficient condition for success in alleviating malnutrition.

Governments may find it worthwhile to support fisheries operations to provide fish to the poor through the market or through feeding programs. From the point of view of government, a small subsidy to a fisheries project might be more beneficial than alternatives such as welfare programs or direct feeding programs. That is, a fisheries project with good nutritional impacts might be understood as a form of nutrition intervention. In that case there would be no presumption that the project would have to yield a positive cash flow.

If estimates could be made of the extent to which any given project helped to alleviate malnutrition (perhaps by estimating the number of persons who were helped to cross some nutritional threshold level), that effectiveness could be assessed as being equivalent in social value to some amount of revenue earnings. It would then become clear that, from the point of view of public policy, the task is to choose projects which yield the best mix of socially important values, and not just to choose the best revenue producer. Thus, placing an explicit value on the alleviation of malnutrition could affect project choices--as it should.

International agencies with responsibilities for the evaluation of fisheries development projects could take the lead in formulating and using sophisticated evaluation models which take the alleviation of malnutrition--along with other important values--fully into account. This would not amount to a rejection of conventional styles of economic analysis. Rather, it would be a matter of broadening those techniques, allowing a fuller range of values to be considered. Projects should be judged according to whether they are gainful overall, and not only according to whether they are profitable in the narrow economic sense.

FISHERIES PROJECT DESIGN

Increasing production, reducing waste, increasing efficiency, supporting small-scale operations, increasing employment, and improving technology are all familiar objectives of fisheries development. None of these will necessarily lead to the alleviation of malnutrition; that should be regarded as a distinct objective in itself, not only in the evaluation but also in the initial design of projects. If it is not given full attention, the pursuit of the more conventional objectives of fisheries development can lead to a deterioration in local nutrition. The development of fish meal processing as a cottage industry,[7] for example, might be an attractive means of economic development for the poor, but such operations could reduce the supplies of fish available for local consumption. Increased use of low value fish does not necessarily yield

low cost products benefiting those most vulnerable to malnutrition.[8] The products are more likely to move toward
the most vigorous commercial markets.

When efficient use of by-catches, trash fish, low
grade fish, and undersized fish is urged, producers and
processors will seek increased efficiency from their perspective, not from the perspective of consumers in general or the needy in particular. "Improvements" may
yield increasing revenue (possibly to a very small number
of individuals), but result in the product's being shipped
away from the poor. Improved preservation techniques,
for example, can make it easier to sell fish to markets
elsewhere, leaving less available for local consumption.

To help assure that positive nutritional impacts are
incorporated, the FAO's guidelines for integrating nutritional considerations into agricultural projects could be
adapted to apply to fisheries projects.[9] Where it is not
possible to conduct the full data collection and analysis
that might be desirable, useful estimates of the likely
nutritional impacts of fisheries projects can be obtained
through interviews with individuals who have good knowledge of the project and its surrounding local conditions.
Such observers may be able to estimate the degree to
which the products are consumed locally, and further, they
may be able to estimate the degree to which local people
depend on those products.

174

NOTES

1. Possibilities for aquaculture's responding to human nutritional needs are explored in Leah H. Smith and Susan Peterson, eds., *Aquaculture Development in Less Developed Countries* (Boulder, Colorado: Westview Press, 1982).
2. Frank Fermin, "The Introduction of Integrated Backyard Farms in Lowland Cavite, Philippines," in I. R. Smith, E. B. Torres, and E. O. Tan, eds., *Philippine Tilapia Economics*, ICLARM Conference Proceedings 12 (Manila: Philippine Council for Agriculture and Resources Research and Development, Los Banos, Laguna, and International Center for Living Aquatic Resources Management, 1985), pp. 151-164.
3. Peter Edwards, Kamtorn Kaewpaitoon, Anussorn Meewan, Anant Harnprasitkam, and Chintana Chantachaeng, *A Feasibility Study of Fish/Duck Integrated Farming at the Family Level in Central and Northeast Thailand* (Bangkok: Asian Institute of Technology, 1983). This study took the opportunity cost of labor to be zero. If an individual has no alternatives which offer cash employment one can say that the opportunity cost of labor is zero--but only in the narrow economic sense. In fact, people in non-cash economies must budget their time very carefully to be sure that it is used gainfully. Working an aquaculture pond draws one away from the vegetable garden. Taking the opportunity cost of labor to be zero fails to recognize one of the most valuable assets such individuals have.
4. C. Peter Timmer, Walter P. Falcon, and Scott R. Pearson, *Food Policy Analysis* (Baltimore: Johns Hopkins University Press/World Bank, 1983), p. 57.

5. E. R. Perez and D. R. Yngente, "Eureka for the Protein Content of Some Fish Species," *Fisheries Today* (Manila), Vol. 2, No. 3 (August 1979), pp. 38-41.
6. James E. Austin and Christopher Mock, "High-Protein Product Development in Thailand," in James E. Austin, *Nutrition Programs in the Third World: Cases and Readings* (Cambridge, Massachusetts: Oelgeschlager, Gunn & Hain, 1981), p. 155.
7. S. Etoh, "Fishmeal from By-Catch on a Cottage Industry Scale" *INFOFISH Marketing Digest*, No. 5 (September 1982), pp. 24-28.
8. Yutaka Hirasawa, "Increasing the Human Consumption of Low-Priced Fish," *INFOFISH Marketing Digest*, No. 1/84 (January/February 1984), pp.17-18.
9. Food and Agriculture Organization of the United Nations, *Integrating Nutrition into Agricultural and Rural Development Projects: A Manual* (Rome: FAO, 1982).

Chapter 11

FISHERIES POLICY

POLICY INTERACTIONS

As Part 2's survey of several different countries has shown, fisheries policy generally is geared to production for the maximization of revenues, increasing foreign exchange earnings, generating employment opportunities, conserving fish stocks for future production, alleviating the poverty of small-scale fishers, and producing domestic food supplies. The market orientation is dominant. Some apparently non-economic (economically inefficient) policies are instituted by governments, however, as in the protection of the interests of small-scale fishers. Given the lack of organization of consumers in relation to this sector, management is guided much more by producer interests than by consumer interests. Fishing is viewed more as a source of government revenue than as a target for its allocation. Allocations to the fisheries sector are regarded as investments which will later return more revenues to the government and to the economy as a whole.

Nutrition programs, in contrast, generally are viewed as welfare programs involving transfer payments to the poor, operating on a non-market basis. They are seen as drains on government revenues, and thus as something to be minimized. It may be acknowledged that there could be some return on "investment" in human capital, but that return is likely to be regarded as small and uncertain.

Fisheries and nutrition policies generally are not in direct conflict. Rather, they are relatively unconnected, operating in different terms and in different realms. As Jesse Floyd observes, in Southeast Asia:

> Fisheries development policies do not explicitly promote fish consumption or take nutrition objectives into account. It is widely believed that it is unnecessary to encourage fish consumption because of the general acceptability of fish and even preference for fish among local populations. Strategies to promote consumption, therefore, are based on programs to introduce fish culture and to reduce prices by increasing supplies, and on policies to increase personal incomes and employment opportunities. Research efforts are underway to identify and produce low-cost products and to convert fishmeal into products for direct human consumption, but there are no specific fisheries programs that give priority to nutrition or that distribute fish to the poor or other population groups at risk of malnutrition.[1]

Those who do the production, processing, and marketing are primarily concerned with benefits and costs to themselves. The role and responsibility of government is to assure that the interests of consumers are taken into account as well. Thus it is a particular responsibility of government to give consideration to the effects of fisheries projects on those most at risk of undernutrition.

Many countries have well developed fisheries but at the same time suffer widespread protein-energy malnutrition, vitamin A deficiency, iron deficiency, and iodine deficiency. Fisheries products can be used to respond to these problems. Cost may at times be an impediment, but often the more significant issue is the need for appropriate policies and programs to assure that suitable products are available where they are needed.

Programs for using fishery products for alleviating malnutrition can be divided into three major types: those which focus on self-provisioning, those which use conventional marketing channels, and those which are based on direct feeding programs. Self-provisioning programs would not benefit established commercial operators, but to the extent that such programs address individuals who are economically or geographically out of reach of commercial markets, they would not hurt the industry either.

Marketing and direct feeding programs can benefit the fishing industry--in its production, processing, and distribution phases--by creating new demand for fisheries products. The benefits can be much greater if governments or other agencies provide some subsidy. In order to help develop local fisheries, food aid agencies might purchase products locally even when they can be imported more cheaply. It is likely that the beneficiaries of such programs would want to continue using fishery products after they conclude their periods of subsidized consumption.

EXPORTS

Fisheries policies can have a considerable impact on nutrition.[2] For example, while national fisheries policies generally are geared to maximizing production (within ecological limits) and thus increasing overall supplies, it makes a difference whether production and processing favor products consumed by the poor or whether they favor products consumed by the middle and upper classes.

From the point of view of the poor there may be little difference between favoring middle and upper classes within the country and favoring customers abroad. Most of the production from relatively poor Palawan in the Philippines, for example, is taken to Manila and other urban centers. In Thailand, "all varieties of food flow to the Central region, especially to those big cities with high purchasing power." One result is that "the price of Pla Tu, a kind of marine fish commonly consumed by the northeastern rural people, was triple that of the Bangkok price."[3]

Some countries have a policy of increasing self-reliance in fish, interpreted as increasing production, reducing imports, and increasing exports. This results in a more favorable balance of trade in terms of increasing foreign exchange reserves. However, if production is not increased significantly, it also reduces the supply of fish available for domestic consumption. Exports in large quantities can reduce supplies available for domestic consumption. They also tend to increase domestic prices, with the result that the supplies which remain available tend to shift toward higher income consumers and become less accessible to the poor. In a number of countries the volume of fisheries products being exported is growing faster than the volume made available for domestic consumption. The foreign exchange that is earned theoretically could be used to purchase cheaper foods for domestic consumption, but often it is not used that way. Thus there are genuine tensions between the need to earn foreign exchange through exports and the need to maintain domestic supplies to serve local nutritional needs, especially the needs of the poor.

In some cases domestic nutritional needs are modest and export prices are high, so the argument for exporting is compelling. In other cases domestic needs may be more significant. In every case an appropriate balance must be struck. Suitable analytical models are needed to help governments in finding that balance. Any such model should provide guidance for determining the extent to which exporting some share of national fisheries production affects nutrition within the country, and it should indicate some means for placing a value on those effects, whether positive or negative.

The model also should differentiate among different types of products. Some, like shrimp, may have a high export price and low domestic demand, while for others the reverse may be true. Thus export policies should be differentiated according to the character of the product. Interactions should be taken into account as well. For example, a strong shrimp export market may draw producers away from supplying products which are important for local consumption.

With these tools it would become possible to evaluate and compare alternative export policies in relation to their nutritional impacts, much as one could evaluate alternative fisheries development projects in relation to their nutritional impacts.

LIAISON

National nutrition agencies may undertake programs such as nutrition education, on-site feeding, take-home feeding, nutrient dense foods, ration shops, food coupons, fortification, direct nutrient dosage, and food processing and distribution activities.[4] While one may want to suggest the establishment of new programs of these types, ordinarily it could not be expected that entirely new activities would be initiated simply to increase the usage of fish. In most cases it would be more practical to suggest adaptations in ongoing programs than to propose new ones.

Given the division of responsibilities among agencies of government, fisheries agencies would not normally be expected to take the initiative regarding nutrition in general or malnutrition in particular. They would not design nutrition programs. However, proposals concerned specifically with the use of fish in nutrition quite properly would come from fisheries agencies.

Programs for increasing the use of fisheries products for the alleviation of malnutrition should be formulated through close cooperation between the fisheries and the nutrition agencies of government. Since the fisheries agencies serve as surrogate suppliers while the nutrition agencies serve as surrogate consumers, the two should be well coordinated. Nutrition agencies can provide guidance regarding what kinds of nutrients are needed where, to help assure that the demand for nutrients is more effectively matched to the supply. Fisheries agencies can help to find or develop products which would be useful in specific nutrition-oriented activities.

This liaison is important not only within national governments but also at the level of local administrative bodies and at the level of international organizations. The communication that has been initiated among the Fisheries Division, the Food Policy and Nutrition Division, and the World Food Programme of the Food and Agriculture Organization of the United Nations could demonstrate the kind of linkage that should be established.

NATIONAL ACTION

With appropriate policy guidance, fisheries agencies working together with nutrition agencies could make a very substantial contribution to alleviating malnutrition. Policy and program initiatives which might be undertaken include the following:

1. Review national fisheries policies to assess their impacts on nutrition, and reorient those policies to help alleviate malnutrition where feasible.

2. Institute strengthened linkages between agencies responsible for fisheries and agencies responsible for nutrition through exchange educational programs and joint committees.

3. Develop and use methods for assessing the nutritional impact of fisheries development projects.

4. Nutrition agencies should keep fisheries agencies informed of the state of nutrition throughout the country and highlight places and ways in which fisheries products might be useful in helping to alleviate malnutrition.

5. Provide increased research and other support for self-provisioning fishing activities by the poor, including both capture and culture.

6. Investigate potentials for stocking lakes and reservoirs in areas where they are likely to be fished for self-provisioning by the poor.

7. Provide increased research and other support for development of seafoods consumed by the poor.

8. Develop the production, processing, and marketing of low cost fisheries products where there is reason to expect that they will be consumed by the poor.

9. Develop nutrition education programs for homemakers to emphasize practical aspects of cooking and preservation of both traditional and novel fisheries products.

10. Promote the use of fisheries products in large-scale institutional feeding programs for those vulnerable to malnutrition, particularly in schools and in hospitals.

11. Review ongoing nutrition programs to identify ways in which fisheries products might be used more effectively.

12. Review the use of "trash" fish to identify ways in which the product might be used for direct human consumption, either directly or in processed form.

13. Review export practices with respect to their effects on domestic nutrition and modify those practices as needed.

14. Develop non-market means of distributing fisheries projects, including social marketing, subsidies, supplemental feeding programs, and institutional feeding programs.

15. Review the possibilities for using fisheries products in both international and domestic food aid programs.

INTERNATIONAL ACTION

The central locus of action for increasing the use of fisheries products for the alleviation of malnutrition should be in national governments. However, regional agencies concerned with the development of fisheries (such as the International Center for Living Aquatic Resources Management, the Southeast Asian Fisheries

Development Center, and INFOFISH) could give more attention to the nutritive potential of fisheries products. There are many initiatives which could be taken by national and international development agencies (such as FAO, the United Nations Development Program, the Canadian International Development Agency, the United States Agency for International Development, the World Bank, and regional development banks such as the Asian Development Bank) to support this action. Such agencies could:

1. Support research to identify and describe programs in which fisheries products have been used effectively to help alleviate malnutrition. For example, a study of "Community-Managed Fish Ponds" would be useful for documenting, comparing, and assessing pond operations in the Philippines, Thailand, Bangladesh, Sri Lanka, Panama, and elsewhere. Casebooks describing such programs could be prepared.

2. Support research on techniques for assessing fisheries development projects which would take nutrition considerations explicitly into account. Sponsor studies of the relative cost-effectiveness of fisheries products in alleviating malnutrition, on a case-study basis.

3. Sponsor an expert consultation to review past experience and to formulate new and improved ways in which fisheries products might be used to alleviate malnutrition.

4. Support the publication of revised and updated versions of Heen and Kreuzer's *Fish in Nutrition* and Borgstrom's *Fish as Food*, with a specific focus on malnutrition.[5]

5. Support the operation of interagency teams through which fisheries agencies and nutrition agencies can collaborate, possibly through a program of grants to support joint programs.

Support pilot projects on the use of fisheries products to alleviate malnutrition.

International banks could provide funds to support the improved use of fisheries products in alleviating malnutrition. Some projects, such as those based on institutional feeding, might be undertaken on the basis of hard loans, with full commercial viability.

MOTIVATING THE ACTION

For centuries fish has made a significant contribution to the alleviation of malnutrition in many parts of the world. Numerous programs to increase the supply of fish generally available for human consumption and to keep its price down have helped to augment that contribution.

However, the process by which supplies are matched to needs has depended on chance and on the vagaries of imperfect markets. The pattern has been to produce low cost fisheries products, put them on the market, and hope that they would be obtained by those who needed them. If fish is to be used more effectively to alleviate malnutrition than it is now, systematic and deliberate efforts would have to be undertaken to connect those most vulnerable to malnutrition with suitable supplies of fisheries products. To strengthen the linkages it is necessary to identify target groups with concretely assessed nutritional deficiencies, to identify particular fisheries products which are available or could be formulated to meet those needs, and to carefully design programs to deliver those products where they are needed, whether through market or nonmarket mechanisms.

Regular linkages could be maintained at the agency level, but initial connections would have to be made higher up, at the policymaking level. Establishing effective liaison between fisheries agencies and nutrition agencies is not simply a matter of coordination. The two agencies begin with very different purposes, and thus at the outset they might not see that there is much to coordinate about. One major reason for establishing a series of meetings at the policymaking level is to build a sense of shared purpose in the common goal of alleviating malnutrition. If that is not established there is not likely to be any meaningful cooperation between the two agencies.

Ideally, the steps would be relatively straightforward. There would have to be a high level policy decision that fisheries products should be used to help alleviate malnutrition. One major step would be to reformulate the objectives of fisheries development to explicitly acknowledge its potential contribution to the alleviation of malnutrition. A formulation something like this might be considered for inclusion in the relevant planning documents:

> The objectives of fisheries development are to increase the production of fish and fisheries products, increase the incomes of workers in the industry, earn foreign exchange, create better opportunities for employment, and contribute to the nation's food supplies, especially for those most at risk of malnutrition.

Activities designed to enhance the use of fisheries in combating malnutrition might be undertaken through a large scale, well publicized program. National fisheries agencies and nutrition agencies then should establish mechanisms for collaboration. The first stage would be a process of mutual education in which fisheries specialists learned in detail about nutritional needs in the country, and in which nutrition specialists learned about the available and potential fisheries supplies. There would then follow an exercise of matching supplies with needs, not on a one-time basis but on the basis of regular--perhaps annual--consultation. Where potential matches were identified, study teams including specialists from both agencies could design concrete programs. Followup studies could be conducted to study the effectiveness of these programs and to modify them as necessary. The two agencies, although pursuing rather different missions, could do a great deal to support one another. The ideal might not be achieved, but even with modest policies and programs, fisheries products could be of much greater help in addressing problems of malnutrition.

NOTES

1. Jesse M. Floyd, *The Role of Fish in Nutrition in Four Selected Countries of Southeast Asia,* Consultant's report prepared for Food Policy and Nutrition Division, FAO, 1984, pp. 80-81.
2. George Kent, "Fisheries and Undernutrition," *Ecology of Food and Nutrition,* Vol. 16 (1985), pp. 281-294; Jesse M. Floyd, *The Political Economy of Fisheries Development in Indonesia, Malaysia, the Philippines, and Thailand* (Honolulu: Doctoral dissertation in Political Science, University of Hawaii, 1985).
3. *Country Report on Impact of Agricultural and Rural Development Projects . . .,* pp. 19-20.
4. This categorization of programs is elaborated in Austin, *Confronting Urban Malnutrition,* and in James E. Austin and Marian F. Zeitlin, eds., *Nutrition Intervention in Developing Countries: An Overview* (Cambridge, Massachusetts: Oelgeschlager, Gunn & Hain, 1981).
5. These studies need revision not only because they are generally outdated but also because they were based on the now-outmoded assumption that the major cause of widespread chronic undernutrition is inadequate protein intake.

BIBLIOGRAPHY

AECOS, Inc./Oceanic Resources, Inc. *Central and Western Pacific Regional Fisheries Development Plan, Vol. 4: Regional Plan.* Honolulu: Pacific Basin Development Council, 1983.

Africa South of the Sahara 1986, Fifteenth Edition. London: Europa Publications, 1985.

Andrae, Gunilla and Beckman, Björn. *The Wheat Trap: Bread and Underdevelopment in Nigeria.* London: ZED Books, 1985.

Annual Report, Fiscal Year 1977. Pago Pago: Office of Samoan Information, Government of American Samoa, 1977.

Asian Development Bank. *Bank Operations in the Fisheries Sector.* Manila: ADB, 1979.

Austin, James E. *Confronting Urban Malnutrition: The Design of Nutrition Programs.* Baltimore: Johns Hopkins University Press/World Bank, 1980.

Austin, James E. and Zeitlin, Marian F., eds. *Nutrition Intervention in Developing Countries: An Overview.* Cambridge, Massachusetts: Oelgeshlager, Gunn & Hain, 1981.

Baluyut, Elvira. *Stocking and Introduction of Fish in Lakes and Reservoirs in the ASEAN (Association of Southeast Asian Nations) Countries.* FAO Fisheries Technical Paper 236. Rome: Food and Agriculture Organization of the United Nations, 1983.

Baxter, Michael W. P. *Food in Fiji: The Produce and Processed Food Distribution Systems.* Canberra: Australian National University, 1980.

Bell, Frederick W. *Food from the Sea: The Economics and Politics of Ocean Fisheries.* Boulder, Colorado: Westview Press, 1978.

Borgstrom, Georg, ed. *Fish as Food.* Four volumes. New York: Academic Press, 1961, 1962, 1965, 1965.

Borgstrom, Georg. *Too Many: A Study of the Earth's Biological Limitations.* New York: Macmillan, 1969.

190

Bruce, Charlotte. "Seaweed as Food," *INFOFISH Marketing Digest*, No. 4/83 (July/August 1983), pp. 27-29.

Bung-Orn Saisithi. "Thailand," in *Fish By-Catch . . . Bonus from the Sea*. Ottawa, Canada: International Development Research Centre/Food and Agriculture Organization of the United Nations, 1982.

Campbell-Asselbergs, Elizabeth. "A Nutritional Approach to Fisheries Projects," *Food and Nutrition*, Vol. 12, No. 2 (1986), pp. 36-44.

Carr, Claudia and Carr, James. "World Hunger: A Solution from the Sea? *Environment*, Vol. 22, No. 1 (January 1980), p. 3.

Cati, A. "Nutrition Problems in Kiribati," in *Report on the First Intersectoral National Nutrition Workshop, 13th-17th June 1983*. Tarawa, Kiribati: USP Centre Teaoraereke. 1983.

Clark, William Fenton. *Population, Agriculture and Urbanization in the Kingdom of Tonga*. East Lansing, Michigan: Ph.D. dissertation, Department of Geography, 1975.

Clay, C. H. *New Reservoirs in Africa, 1980-2000*. Rome: FAO CIFA Occasional Paper No. 11, 1984.

Coche, André and Demoulin, François. *Report of the Workshop on Aquaculture Planning in the Southern African Development Coordination (SADCC) Countries*. Rome: FAO CIFA Technical Paper No. 15, 1986.

Coyne, Terry (with editing by Jacqui Badcock and Richard Taylor). *The Effect of Urbanization and Western Diet on the Health of Pacific Island Populations*. Noumea, New Caledonia: South Pacific Commission, 1984.

Dixon, John A. and Tyers, Rodney. "India's Food Security: Supply, Demand, and Signs of Success," in Anthony H. Chisholm and Rodney Tyers, eds., *Food Security: Theory, Policy, and Perspectives from Asia and the Pacific Rim*. Lexington, Massachusetts: Lexington Books, 1982.

Edwards, Peter; Kamtorn Kaewpaitoon; Anussorn Meewan; Anant Harnprasitkam; and Chintana Chantachaeng. *A Feasibility Study of Fish/Duck Integrated Farming at the Family Level in Central and Northeast*

Thailand. Bangkok: Asian Institute of Technology, 1983.

Etoh, S. "Fishmeal from By-Catch on a Cottage Industry Scale," *INFOFISH Marketing Digest*, No. 5 (September 1982), pp. 24-28.

Expert Committee on Ciguatera, *Report of Meeting.* Noumea, New Caledonia: South Pacific Commission, 1981.

FAO World Conference on Fisheries Management and Development. *Draft Strategy for Fisheries Management and Development and Associated Programs of Action.* Rome: FAO, 1984.

Fermin, Frank. "The Introduction of Integrated Backyard Farms in Lowland Cavite, Philippines," in I. R. Smith, E. B. Torres, and E. O. Tan, eds., *Philippine Tilapia Economics, ICLARM Conference Proceedings 12.* Manila: Philippine Council for Agriculture and Resources Research and Development, Los Banos, Laguna, and International Center for Living Aquatic Resources Management, 1985.

Fine, John C. "Progress Toward Tradition," *Oceans*, Vol. 17, No. 6 (November-December 1984), pp. 24-26.

Finney, Ben R. "Economic Change and Dietary Consequences Among the Tahitians," *Micronesia*, Vol. 2, No. 1 (June 1965), pp. 1-14.

First Nationwide Nutrition Survey, Philippines, 1978 (Summary Report). Manila: Food and Nutrition Institute, National Science Board, 1979.

Floyd, J. M. *The Political Economy of Fisheries Development in Indonesia, Malaysia, the Philippines, and Thailand.* Honolulu: Doctoral Dissertation in Political Science, University of Hawaii, 1985.

Food and Agriculture Organization of the United Nations, Committee on Agriculture. *Malnutrition: Its Nature, Magnitude and Policy Implications.* Rome: FAO COAG, December 1982.

Food and Agriculture Organization of the United Nations. *A Framework for the Formulation and Implementation of a National Fishery Policy in Tanzania.* Rome: FAO/Norway Cooperative Program, 1984.

Food and Agriculture Organization of the United Nations. *Integrating Nutrition into Agricultural and Rural*

Development Projects: A Manual. Rome: FAO, 1982.

Food and Agriculture Organization of the United Nations. *1983 Yearbook of Fishery Statistics: Catches and Landings.* Rome: FAO, 1984.

Food and Agriculture Organization of the United Nations. *1983 Yearbook of Fishery Statistics: Fishery Commodities.* Rome: FAO, 1984.

Food and Agriculture Organization of the United Nations. *The Potential of Fisheries in Alleviating Undernutrition. Report of the Discussions and Conclusions of an Expert Consultation on the Role of Fish and Fisheries in World Nutrition.* FAO Fisheries Circular No. 761. Rome: FAO, 1983.

Food and Agriculture Organization of the United Nations. *Report of the FAO World Conference on Fisheries Management and Development, Rome 27 June to 6 July 1984.* Rome: FAO, 1984.

Food and Agriculture Organization of the United Nations. *FAO Workshop on National Preparedness for Acute and Large-Scale Food Shortages in Asia and the Pacific. Bangkok, 2-6 May 1983.* Rome: FAO, 1983.

Food and Agriculture Organization of the United Nations. *The Fourth World Food Survey.* Rome: FAO, 1977.

Food and Agriculture Organization of the United Nations. *The Fifth World Food Survey.* Rome: FAO, 1985.

Food and Agriculture Organization of the United Nations. *Fishery Products and the Consumer in Developing Countries,* FAO Fisheries Report No. 271. Rome: FAO, 1983.

Food and Agriculture Organization of the United Nations, Regional Office for Asia and the Pacific. *Food Consumption in the Asia-Pacific Region 1972-1982.* Bangkok: FAO, RAPA, 1985.

Garcia Perez, Alan. "Peru Wants an Historic Re-Encounter With Its Land," *IFDA Dossier, No. 52* (March/April 1986), pp. 17–28.

Glucksman, Joe. "Papua New Guinea's Sepik River Salt Fish Industry," *South Pacific Commission Fisheries Newsletter,* No. 17 (December 1978), pp. 22–28.

Government of India. *Seventh Five Year Plan, 1985-90,*

Vol. II. New Delhi: Planning Commission, 1985.
Government of India. *Sixth Five Year Plan, 1980-85.* New Delhi: Planning Commission, 1981.
Grant, James P. *The State of the World's Children 1981-82.* New York: United Nations Children's Fund, 1982.
Gulati, Leela. *Women in Fishing Villages on the Kerala Coast: Demographic and Socio-Economic Impacts of a Fisheries Development Project.* Geneva: World Employment Programme Working Paper No. 128, International Labour Organisation, 1983.
Gupta, V. K. et al. *Marine Fish Marketing in India*, Volumes I-VI. Ahmedabad: Indian Institute of Management, 1984.
Hamnett, Michael P.; Surber, Russ J.; Surber, Denise E.; and Denoncour, Mark T. "Economic Vulnerability in the Pacific," in John Carter, ed. *Pacific Islands Yearbook*, 15th Edition. Sydney: Pacific Publications, 1984.
Hau'ofa, E. *Corned Beef and Tapioca: A Report on the Food Distribution Systems in Tonga.* Suva, Fiji: Centre for Applied Studies in Development, University of the South Pacific, 1978.
Heen, Eirik and Kreuzer, Rudolf, eds. *Fish in Nutrition.* London: Fishing News (Books) Ltd., 1962.
Heslinga, G. A. and Perron, F. E. "The Status of Giant Clam Mariculture Technology in the Indo-Pacific," *South Pacific Commission Fisheries Newsletter*, No. 24 (January-March 1983), pp. 15-19.
Hill, Harry Burnette. *The Use of Nearshore Marine Life as a Food Resource by American Samoans.* Honolulu: Pacific Islands Program Working Papers, 1978.
Hokama, Yoshitsugi and Miyahara, James T. "Ciguatera Poisoning: Clinical and Immunological Aspects," *Journal of Toxicology: Toxins Review*, Vol. 5, No. 1 (1986), pp. 25-54.
Holt, Sidney. "Marine Fisheries," in Elisabeth Mann Borgese and Norton Ginsburg, eds., *Ocean Yearbook 1.* Chicago: University of Chicago Press, 1978.
Howard, Michael C.; Plange, Nii-K.; Durutalo, Simione; and Witton, Ron. *The Political Economy of the South Pacific.* Townsville, Australia: James Cook

194

University South East Asian Monograph Series Number 13, 1983.

Idyll, Clarence P. *The Sea Against Hunger: Harvesting the Oceans to Feed a Hungry World*, Revised Edition. New York: Thomas Y. Crowell Co., 1978.

Indo-Pacific Fishery Commission (IPFC). *Report of the Joint Workshop of the IPFC Working Party on Inland Fisheries and the IPFC Working Party on Aquaculture on the Role of Stocking and Introductions in the Improvement of Production of Lakes and Reservoirs, New Delhi, India, 24-25 January 1984.* Rome: Food and Agriculture Organization of the United Nations, 1984.

Irrigation in Africa South of the Sahara. Rome: FAO Investment Center Technical Paper 5, 1985.

James, David. "The Future for Fish in Nutrition," *INFOFISH Marketing Digest*, No. 4 (1984), pp. 41-44.

James, David. "The Prospects for Fish for the Malnourished," *Food and Nutrition*, Vol. 12, No. 2 (1986), pp. 20-30.

Johannes, R. E. *Words of the Lagoon: Fishing and Marine Lore in the Palau District of Micronesia.* Berkeley: University of California Press, 1981.

Josepeit, Helga. *The Economic and Social Effects of the Fishing Industry: A Comparative Study.* Rome: FAO Fisheries Circular No. 314, Revision 1, 1981.

Kapetsky, J. M. and Petr, T. *Status of African Reservoir Fisheries.* Rome: FAO CIFA Technical Paper No. 10, 1984.

Kearney, R. E. "Fishery Potentials in the Tropical Central and Western Pacific," *South Pacific Commission Fisheries Newsletter*, No. 24 (January-March 1983), pp. 20-31.

Kearney, R. E. "Some Economic Aspects of the Development and Management of Fisheries in the Central and Western Pacific," *South Pacific Commission Fisheries Newsletter*, No. 22 (July 1981), pp. 6-15.

Kent, George. *The Politics of Pacific Island Fisheries.* Boulder, Colorado: Westview Press, 1980.

Kent, George. *Transnational Corporations in Pacific Fishing.* Sydney: Transnational Corporations Research Project, 1980.

Kent, George. "Food Trade: The Poor Feed the Rich," *Food and Nutrition Bulletin*, Vol. 4, No. 4 (October 1982), pp. 25-33.

Kent, George. "The Pattern of Fish Trade," *ICLARM Newsletter*, Vol. 6, No. 2 (April 1983), pp. 12-13.

Kent, George. *The Political Economy of Hunger: The Silent Holocaust*. New York: Praeger, 1984.

Kent, George. *National Fishery Policies and the Alleviation of Malnutrition in the Philippines and Thailand*. Rome: FAO Fisheries Circular No. 777, 1984.

Kent, George. "Fisheries and Undernutrition," *Ecology of Food and Nutrition*, Vol. 16 (1985), pp. 281-294.

Kent, George. "Aquaculture: Motivating Production for Low-Income Markets," and "Sharing the Catch at Village Level: Fish-Ponds in Thailand," *Ceres*, Vol. 19, No. 4 (July-August 1986), pp. 23-27.

Kent, George. "Impacts of Fisheries Policy," *Food and Nutrition*, Vol. 12, No. 2 (1986), pp. 32-35.

Koester, Ulrich. *Regional Cooperation to Improve Food Security in Southern and Eastern African Countries*. Washington, D.C.: International Food Policy Research Institute, 1986.

Krone, Wolfgang. "Fish as Food: Present Contribution and Potential," *Food Policy*, Vol. 4 (November 1979), pp. 259-268.

Kurien, John. *Pisiculture Potentials in Dharmapuri District, Tamilnadu*. Trivandrum: Centre for Development Studies, 1983.

Lambert, Julian. "The Effect of Urbanization and Western Foods on Infant and Maternal Nutrition in the South Pacific," *Food and Nutrition Bulletin*, Vol. 4, No. 3 (July 1982), pp. 11-13.

Lands, William E. M. *Fish and Human Health*. Orlando, Florida: Academic Press, 1986.

Lewis, Nancy Davis. "Ciguatera in the Pacific: Incidence and Implications for Marine Resource Development," in Edward Ragelis, ed., *Seafood Toxins*. Washington, D.C.: American Chemical Society, 1984.

Lewis, Nancy Davis. "Ciguatera--Parameters of a Tropical Health Problem," *Human Ecology*, Vol. 12, No. 3 (1984), pp. 253-273.

Lindsey, C. C. *Fisheries Training in the Region Served by the University of the South Pacific*. Suva:

University of the South Pacific, 1972.

Livesey, C. H. "Food Imports," *Pacific Islands Monthly*, July 1976, p. 23.

Lucas, Kenneth C. "World Fisheries Management: A Time to Build," *Vital Speeches of the Day*, XLV (1979), pp. 740-744.

Luna, Julio. "Fishery Resources," in *Natural Resources in Latin America*. Washington, D.C.: Inter-American Development Bank, 1983.

Luna, Julio, ed. *Non-Traditional Fish Products for Massive Human Consumption*. Washington, D.C.: Inter-American Development Bank, 1981.

Lunven, Paul. "The Role of Fish in Human Nutrition," *Food and Nutrition*, Vol. 8, No. 2 (1982), pp. 9-18.

Marshall, B. E. *Small Pelagic Fishes and Fisheries in African Inland Waters*. Rome: CIFA Technical Paper No. 14, 1984.

May, R. C. *South Pacific Agricultural Survey 1979: Sector Paper on Fisheries*. Manila: Asian Development Bank, 1979.

McLaren, D. S. "The Great Protein Fiasco," *Lancet*, Vol. 2 (1974), pp. 93-96.

Mellor, John W. *The New Economics of Growth--A Strategy for India and the Developing World*. Ithaca, New York: Cornell University Press, 1976.

Meltzoff, Sarah K. and LiPuma, Edward S. *A Japanese Fishing Joint Venture: Worker Experience and National Development in the Solomon Islands*. Manila: International Center for Living Aquatic Resources Management, 1983.

Moorsom, Richard. *Exploiting the Sea*. London: The Catholic Institute for International Relations, 1984.

Munro, John L. "Giant Clams--Food for the Future," *ICLARM Newsletter*, Vol. 6, No. 1 (January 1983), pp. 3-4.

National Academy of Sciences. *Supporting Papers: World Food and Nutrition Study*, Volume I. Washington, D.C.: NAS, 1977.

National Forum for Catamaran & Country-Boat Fishermen's Rights & Marine Wealth. "India--Ban Anti-national Multi-million Fishing Complex at Colaba, Bombay, or Anywhere Else in India," *For a Society Overcoming Domination: International Study Days,*

Case Study 1122. Paris: Support Service for Intercommunication, 1980.

National Marine Fisheries Service. *Fisheries of the United States 1985.* Washington, D.C.: NMFS, 1986.

National Marine Fisheries Service. *Imports and Exports of Fishery Products, Annual Summary 1985.* Washington, D.C.: NMFS, 1986.

National Nutrition Council, *Food Policy and Nutrition Plan.* Manila: NNC, 1980.

Neal, Richard A. and Smith, Ian R. "Key Problems in Aquaculture Development," *ICLARM Newsletter,* Vol. 3 (1982), pp. 3-5.

Oliver, Douglas. *Aspects of Modernization in Bougainville, Papua New Guinea.* Honolulu: Pacific Islands Studies, University of Hawaii, 1981.

Omawale. "Kicking the Wheat Habit," *Pan American Health,* Vol. 8, No. 12 (1976), pp. 12-15.

Organisation for Economic Co-operation and Development. *International Trade in Fish Products: Effects of the 200-Mile Limit.* Paris: OECD, 1982.

Oswald, E. O. *Seventh Technical Meeting on Fisheries.* Noumea, New Caledonia: South Pacific Commission, July 1974.

Otang, Tion. "Nutrition in the Primary School," in *Report on the First Intersectoral National Nutrition Workshop, 13th-17th June 1983.* Tarawa, Kiribati: USP Centre Teaoraereke. 1983.

Pariser, E. R. and Ruckes, E. *Non-Traditional Foods from Fish for Institutional Markets (Ecuador-Peru-Chile-Brazil).* Washington, D.C.: Inter-American Development Bank, 1983.

Pariser, E. R. et al. *Fish Protein Concentrate: Panacea for Protein Malnutrition?* Cambridge, Massachusetts: MIT Press, 1978.

Parkinson, Susan. "Nutrition in the South Pacific--Past and Present," *Journal of Food and Nutrition,* Vol. 39, No. 3 (1982), pp. 121-125.

Pascual, Conrad R. "Nutrition in the Philippines," in Donald S. McLaren, ed., *Nutrition in the Community.* New York: Wiley, 1976.

Perez, E. R. and Yngente, D. R. "Eureka for the Protein Content of Some Fish Species," *Fisheries Today*

(Manila), Vol. 2, No. 3 (August 1979), pp. 38-41.

Pierce, Barry A. *Ecological Studies of Semi-Intensive Prawn Aquaculture Ponds.* Honolulu: Doctoral Dissertation in Oceanography, University of Hawaii, 1984.

Popma, T. J.; Ross, F. E.; Nerrie, B. L.; and Bowman, J. R. *The Development of Commercial Farming of Tilapia in Jamaica 1979-1983.* Auburn University, Alabama: Alabama Agricultural Experiment Station, 1984.

Popper, D. M. *Fiji Fish Culture.* Rome: Food and Agriculture Organization of the United Nations, 1977.

Quinn, Norman J.; Kojis, Barbara; and Warpeha, Paul. *Subsistence Fishing Practices of Papua New Guinea.* Lae, Papua New Guinea: Appropriate Technology Development Institute, 1984.

Qureshi, Rahmat U. *Nutrition Considerations in Agriculture.* Bangkok: FAO Regional Office for Asia and the Pacific, 1982.

Rabanal, H. R. "Aquaculture in Asia and the Pacific," *INFOFISH Marketing Digest,* No. 1/83 (January/February 1983), pp. 16-18.

Rao, V. K. R. V. *Food, Nutrition, and Poverty in India.* New Delhi: Vikas Publishing House, 1982.

Republic of the Marshall Islands. *First Five Year Development Plan, 1985-1989.* Majuro, Marshall Islands: Nitijela Paper No. 1, 1984.

Robinson, M. A. *Prospects for World Fisheries to 2000.* Rome: Food and Agriculture Organization of the United Nations, 1982.

Rody, Nancy. "Things Go Better With Coconuts: Program Strategies in Micronesia," *Journal of Nutrition Education,* Vol. 10, No. 1 (January-March, 1978), pp. 19-22.

Rody, Nancy. "Consumerism in Micronesia," *South Pacific Bulletin,* Vol. 28 (1978), pp. 9-14.

Rural Fishculture Development and Technology Transfer in Eastern and Southern Africa. Rome: Economic Commission for Africa and FAO, 1985.

Sada, Masayoshi. "Fish Calcium," *INFOFISH Marketing Digest,* No. 1/84 (January/February 1984), pp. 29-30.

Samson, Elizabeth. "Fisheries," in George Kent and

Mark J. Valencia, eds., *Marine Policy in Southeast Asia*. Berkeley: University of California Press, 1984.

Shah, C. H.; Sawant, S. D.; and Sanghavi, B. I. *Nutrition Gap: An Economic Analysis*. Bombay: Himalaya Publishing House, 1983.

Shrimps: A Survey of the World Market. Geneva: International Trade Centre UNCTAD/GATT, 1983.

Simoons, F. J. "Fish as Forbidden Food," *Ecology of Food and Nutrition*, Vol. 3 (1974), pp. 185-201.

Slavin, Joseph. "Review of US Seafood Market," *INFOFISH Marketing Digest*, No. 2/84 (March/April 1984), p. 22.

Smith, Leah H. and Peterson, Susan, eds. *Aquaculture Development in Less Developed Countries*. Boulder, Colorado: Westview Press, 1982.

Solomon Islands National Development Plan, 1985-1989. Honiara: Ministry of Economic Planning, 1985.

Southern African Development Coordination Conference. *SADCC Agriculture: Toward 2000*. Rome: Food and Agriculture Organization of the United Nations, 1984.

Srivastava, U. K. and Reddy, M. Dharma, eds. *Fisheries Development in India: Some Aspects of Policy Management*. New Delhi: Concept Publishing Company, 1983.

Sukhatme, P. V. "Human Protein Needs and the Relative Role of Energy and Protein in Meeting Them," in F. Steele and A. Bourne, eds., *The Man/Food Equation, Proceedings of a Symposium Held at the Royal Institution London, September, 1973*. London: Academic Press, 1975, pp. 53-75.

Sukhatme, P. V. "The Protein Problem: Its Size and Nature," *Journal of the Royal Statistical Society*, Series A, Vol. 137 (1974), pp. 166-200.

Sukhatme, P. V., ed. *New Concepts in Nutrition and Their Implications for Policy*. Pune: Maharashtra Association for the Cultivation of Science, 1982.

Tagle, Maria A.; Valand, S.; and James, D. B. "Acceptability Testing of FPC Type B in Selected Developing Areas," in *Proceedings of the Conference on Handling, Processing, and Marketing of Tropical Fish*. London: Tropical Products Institute, 1977.

Teutscher, Frans, "Fish, Food and Nutrition," *Food and Nutrition*, Vol. 12, No. 2 (1986), pp. 2-10.

Thaman, R. R. "Deterioration of Traditional Food Systems, Increasing Malnutrition and Food Dependency in the Pacific Islands," *Journal of Food and Nutrition*, Vol. 39, No. 3 (1982), pp. 109-121.

Thaman, R. R. and Clarke, W. C. eds. *Food and National Development in the South Pacific*. Suva, Fiji: University of the South Pacific, 1983.

Timmer, C. Peter; Falcon, Walter P.; and Pearson, Scott R. *Food Policy Analysis*. Baltimore: Johns Hopkins University Press/World Bank, 1983.

Uwate, K. Roger; Kunatuba, Peniasi; Raobati, Baraniko; and Tenakanai, Charles. *A Review of Aquaculture Activities in the Pacific Islands Region*. Honolulu: Pacific Islands Development Program, East-West Center, 1984.

Valand, S. "Fish Protein Concentrate Type B--A More Promising Approach," *Food and Nutrition*, Vol. 5, No. 2 (1979), pp. 24-30.

Vanderpuye, C. J. *Evaluation Guidelines for Rational Planning and Management of Tropical and Subtropical Inland Fisheries Under Constraints from Other Uses of Land and Water Resources: Africa*. Rome: FAO Fisheries Circular No. 789, 1985.

Van Heel, Catherina. "Village Fishponds in Thailand," *Food and Nutrition*, Vol. 12, No. 2 (1986), pp. 44-47.

Van Pel, H. *Fish Preservation Simplified*. Noumea, New Caledonia: South Pacific Commission, [1960].

World Bank. *Aspects of Poverty in the Philippines: A Review and Assessment*. Washington, D.C.: WB, 1980.

World Bank. *Fishery Sector Policy Paper*. Washington, D.C.: WB, 1982.

World Bank, *Poverty and Hunger: Issues and Options for Food Security in Developing Countries*. Washington, D.C.: WB, 1986.

World Bank. *World Development Report 1986*. New York: Oxford University Press, 1986.

World Food Programme. *World Food Programme Assistance for Fisheries Development in Third World Countries and The Use of Fish Products in Food Aid*.

Rome: WFP, 1984.

Zeitlin, Marian F. and Formacion, Candelaria S. *Nutrition Intervention in Developing Countries: Study II, Nutrition Education.* Cambridge, Massachusetts: Oelgeschlager, Gunn & Hain, 1981.